In loving memory of

ראובן ברוך בן משה צבי הירש

who exemplified מדות טובות to the
fullest extent.
His uncompromised belief in Hashem
allowed him to keep his spirits up, even
during the most difficult and painful
moments of his life.
Reuvan demonstrated what it means to be
a true Chossid, always with a smile,
he made everyone who came to visit him
feel at home.

Passed away on his birthday - כ"ב אדר תשס"ז

Dedicated by Reuvan's friends

Zalman Ruderman

Adventures in 3D

Publishers & Distributors

Adventures in 3D

ISBN: 978-1661-290-641
First Edition - Iyar 5773 / May 2013
Second Edition - Teves 5780 / Jan 2020

Translation: Yaakov Paley
Illustrations: Yaakov Yarchi
Layout and Design: BSD Publishers
Editorial Assistance: Rivkie Bergstein, Sheina Herz
Managing Editor: Mendy Weiss

Published and Distributed by:
BSD Publishers
Brooklyn, NY
347-560-9770
Info@BSDpublishers.com
www.BSDpublishers.com

Printed in China

Table of Contents

Alex the Beggar

Tell me, have you ever been to an optician for an eye exam? Did the optician set a pair of dim lenses over your eyes? Did he then ask you to tell him which object stood out of a chart hanging on the wall far across the room? The green line or the red line? Or a certain letter or shape? If this ever happened to you, then you know what three-dimensional glasses are.

Normally, when we look at a book or magazine, we only see two dimensions – the length (or height) and the width. But when you wear special glasses, like those we have just described, we notice a third dimension – the depth. All of a sudden, the sky on the horizon seems to slide further away into the distance, while the bird flying from the tree branch directly towards us seems so very close. Everything seems more real.

Why am I telling you all this? Because life is also that way. Most of the time we look too quickly and simply at the people and events around us. We do not gaze or think deeply at what we see. If someone shows us an angry face, for example, we are convinced that he is angry with us. If he smiles, we assume that he likes us.

For a long time now, I have trained myself to look differently at my surroundings. I do not simply accept things the way they first appear. I try to see what might lay behind them. So when the teacher yells at me for no good reason (not that it happens too often, mind you), I keep in mind that perhaps something else – nothing to do with me – made him upset that day, and that he was simply letting out his frustration on me. When someone begins to flatter and praise me without good reason, I immediately begin to wonder whether he might be trying to get something from me. Whenever I see people, adults or children, I enjoy trying to figure out what might really be going on with them.

After a while, I succeeded in creating my own inner set of three-dimensional glasses like the optician uses – looking deeply into things. I began to sense what was going on behind the scene. You could only imagine what I have seen since then… Let me tell you, the real world is far different than what you would expect.

Ever since I was a young boy, I loved to consider the different people I knew or met. I especially examined the way they acted. When I would see a man running to catch a bus, for example, I would try to figure out from his clothing, movement, and the expression on his face, whether he was rushing because he was very busy – or whether he just received an urgent message that required him to arrive at a certain place very quickly. Was he just running late that day or was it an unexpected emergency?

If I saw a mother walking with her children in the street and speaking very kindly and gently to them, I would ask myself whether she is always so patient with her children – or whether she only acts pleasantly when there are other adults around to see her…

If I saw a man crossing a street, heading towards a row of closed stores with a key in his hand, I would try to determine which store he was about to open.

At first, it was just an interest, a hobby. But as time went on, I became an expert. While my friends would play tag or some other game, I would sit and watch the people passing by.

What motivates me to do this, you wonder? Well, I think it is just my nature. My father always tells me that I am a young investigator. Sometimes I wonder whether that might be a polite way to suggest that I am a little nosy...

What really got me investigating everything was a series of interesting events. Thinking about them led me to some surprising discoveries.

The first event, if I am not mistaken, had to do with "Alex the Beggar" – that's how we all referred to him.

One fine sunny day, Alex the Beggar arrived in our neighborhood out of nowhere. He appeared at the local *shul* and began collecting donations. At first, he seemed no different than any of the other paupers who would come to town and stay a while, only to leave and then return again at a later date, before disappearing once more… You know how it is with those collectors.

But Alex was unlike the others. He quickly let it be known that he was here to stay. Within the first week, people were already whispering among themselves about the beggar who had come to settle in the *shul.*

"Who is that man?" they asked each other in surprise.
"How did he land here?" they wondered.

"Does he have family?"
"Does he have a home?"
"Where did he stay until now?"

Dozens of questions swirled around the new beggar, but no one had any answers.

By the second week, we were used to seeing Alex in the *shul* constantly. After three weeks, he had become part of the *shul* furniture. Ever since then, Alex has remained in our *shul.*

I immediately took note of the fact that he was called Alex. That was one of the only things that he agreed to disclose. "My name is Alex," he would respond, with a stammer and a heavy Russian accent.

It was not just his silence that made him appear strange and mysterious. His clothes were always clean and neat. It was clear that some person was secretly taking care of him. At night, he would sleep in one of the small side rooms that branched off from the main hall of our large *shul.* In the morning, when the first *minyan* prepared to begin *davening*, Alex was already up and walking between the congregants. He stared at each person with his two great bulging eyes and he jingled some coins in his hand. That is exactly what he did with all of the later *minyanim* as well.

When all the *minyanim* had finished, Alex would take a seat at one of the long tables in the *shul* and arrange the coins he had collected that morning into neat stacks. One pile for half-*shekels*, another for whole *shekels*… Once he had arranged them into towers and carefully counted their exact number, he would slowly place each pile into a different nylon bag.

Time passed, but nobody could discover anything more about the true identity or personal life of Alex. People spread all sorts of rumors. Some said he was a new immigrant to Israel from Russia. Others insisted that he came to Israel years ago but had never really managed to settle in. One person even suggested that Alex was not really Jewish altogether, but had arrived from Russia with one of the large wave of Jewish immigrants. He quickly realized that by pretending to be a poor Jew, he could collect more money. Well, Alex certainly knew that no one would think of throwing him out of *shul*. In fact, no one ever saw Alex put on *tefillin* or *daven*. Perhaps he *davened* when there was no one around to see him?

For two and a half years, Alex lived in our *shul* and carefully guarded his past. Then came the exciting festival of *Simchas Torah*. In our *shul*, *Simchas Torah* is celebrated with a traditional giant *kiddush*. That year, Alex the Beggar gulped down a fantastic amount of wine and liquor.

• • •

We sat down around the large table that was filled with all sorts of wonderful food. The Rabbi gave his traditional *Simchas Torah* speech and we listened carefully. Our Rabbi, by the way, is famous not only for his great knowledge of Torah, but also for his amazing storytelling. He has an endless storehouse of moving stories. For every situation and topic, he has the perfect matching story. What is even more impressive is that all of these stories are true, real life accounts.

As the Rabbi describes a scene in one of his stories, his white beard trembles slightly, his eyes open wide, and two lights seem to shine forth from his pupils. The story becomes alive and we are drawn into the action.

When not in his presence, we all refer to the Rabbi simply as "Reb Elleh," a short version of his real name, Rabbi Eliyahu. This is by no means a sign of disrespect, quite the opposite, it is meant as a sign of the great affection that we all feel for our Rabbi.

Well, that *Simchas Torah* the Rabbi spoke about the need for *mesiras nefesh* for Torah study, giving up everything for the goal of learning Torah. He then began relating a story, and we all listened closely:

"Everyone knew him as Mottel Kremenchuger because he came from the Russian town of Kremenchug. His real name was Rabbi Mordechai Zaltzman. Have you ever heard of him?

"Let me tell you, I merited getting to know this Reb Mottel when I was a boy of nine or ten years old. Mottel arrived suddenly in our town one day. Did I say 'arrived?' No, he escaped to our town. He escaped from the KGB. They were desperately trying to arrest him because Mottel had organized a network of secret schools to teach people Torah."

The Rabbi closed his eyes for a few moments and thought deeply. He seemed to be traveling swiftly along a vast track of memories.

"For a few weeks, Mottel hid in our house. For my parents, hiding Reb Mottel in our home required amazing courage. In those days, someone caught helping a 'criminal' escape the evil hands of the KGB was treated no less severely than the actual 'criminal.' We were told that if the KGB would catch Mottel, *chas v'sholom*, they would sentence him to death – or at the very least, to tens of years of harsh labor in the far, frozen Siberia, from which few prisoners ever returned. But despite the great danger to themselves, my parents agreed to provide Mottel with a place to hide in our home.

"Mottel was a special person. He was an outstanding Torah scholar, who used every spare moment for the study of Torah. And when Mottel would *daven*… Why, on a regular weekday morning, his *shachris* would last three hours. His prayers were incredibly powerful and heartwarming. He would plead with the Creator with great intensity and sweetness. Reb Mottel also had enormous *yiras shomayim,* fear of Heaven.

"In those days people were literally starving for a piece of bread. Mottel himself had become so thin that you could see his bones. Although his life was in danger every second, he insisted on only eating food with the highest levels of *kashrus*. He would not eat in every house in which he was forced to hide. But he readily agreed to eat the food prepared by my mother. He would say, 'I completely trust the food cooked by the daughter of Avremel the *shochet*!' – that's how he called my grandfather Avraham.

"But in the end," the Rabbi continued sadly, "What do you think happened? The KGB managed to catch Reb Mottel. They dragged him away and for a short time, they interrogated and tortured him in one of their dungeons in Petersburg. After that, they sent him to Siberia. He was never heard of again… Until today, nobody knows when and under what circumstances his holy soul left this earth."

The Rabbi fell silent for a moment as we all held our breath. In a slightly choked voice, he continued. "What is especially painful is that Reb Mottel had a son, an only child who was forced to grow up without a father from the age of five.

"I did not know him personally, but I was told that when he was still young, this son of Reb Mottel Kremenchuger ran away from the home of his mother, who passed away a few years later from her great agony. He went to live among the non-Jews.

"This was Reb Mottel's only son, the only person in the world left to say *kaddish* in the merit of his soul after he died. But Reb Mottel, who sacrificed his own life in order to study and teach Torah and keep the *mitzvos* – his only *'Kaddish'* was lost, gone..."

From the far end of the table, we all heard a muffled sob. Alex the Beggar looked like he was about to burst into tears. Those around him threw him a look of pity. "He must have drunk a little too much liquor," said the wealthy Reb Dovid with a smile. Those around him nodded their heads in agreement.

Suddenly, Alex stood up tall and straight. He called out loudly, *"NYET!"*

Our surprise at this sudden outburst was nothing compared to our complete amazement at Alex's words over the course of the next few minutes.

Alex opened his usually silent mouth and began to speak. "No!" he breathed heavily. "I am Alexander Saltzman, the son of Mottel Kremenchuger, whom the Rabbi just spoke about!"

By now, the crowded *shul* was completely silent. We all stared in shock, as with a broken Hebrew mixed with words of Russian and Yiddish, Alex the Beggar told us his unbelievable story.

Like so many young people in those days, he had fallen for the ideals of communist propaganda. For many years, Alex considered himself a very clever man, and he ridiculed all those Jews who stubbornly clung to their old-fashioned beliefs. He rose through the ranks of the Communist Party and at one point, he was appointed to the position of Chief Secretary of the Dnepropetrovsk branch of the Communist Party. He became so devoted to communism that he completely abandoned regular life. He never married and had no plans to raise a family.

His life continued that way for many years, until the collapse of the Soviet Union. When communism rule fell apart, Alex suddenly found himself completely lost. He had cut himself off from his Jewish roots and his entire life in the Communist Party rapidly disintegrated.

When the gates of the Soviet Union were flung wide open and many Russian Jews began streaming to Israel, the Jewish spark within him began to flicker. He began to seriously consider moving to Israel.

An ironic smile spread across Alex's face as he told the crowded *shul* how the Israeli Consulate in his city demanded that he prove that he was in fact a Jew.

"Vi panimayetzi?" boomed Alex, "do you understand what I am saying? I, the son of Mottel Kremenchuger, had to prove *az ich bin a yid*, that I am Jewish!"

Alex described how from the first moment that he arrived in Israel, he had wandered from one place to the next. He did not speak Hebrew and he had no relatives or friends to turn to for help. He ended up traveling about and collecting donations.

Alex told us that he did not have many memories from his parents' home, but he clearly remembered *Simchas Torah*. He remembered that it was such a happy day, which is why he now made a point of drinking a lot of wine and liquor every *Simchas Torah* to help him forget his troubles and perhaps even feel a little joy.

"I heard you just now speaking about my father, Reb Mottel. You said that his *'Kaddish'* was lost, gone… And so I am telling you for a second time – *NYET!* No! I am the *'Kaddish'* of Mottel Kremenchuger!"

Well, you can only imagine how moved we were by the amazing words of Alex the Beggar, who instantly became Alexander Saltzman.

• • •

If I remember correctly, Alex's story was when I first became aware that things are not all they seem to be. When we look around us, everything seems so simple and smooth. We think that whatever we see with our eyes is all that there is to know. The truth, however, is often far different from what we imagine. Well, if that was the first time I noticed this, it certainly was not the last...

The Importer

In the last story, I briefly mentioned the wealthy Rabbi Dovid. Now, allow me to tell you a little bit about him.

No one in the community calls him "the wealthy Rabbi Dovid," but simply "Reb Dovid." Some go out of their way to call him "*HaRav* Leiner" (Leiner is his last name). To the best of my knowledge, Rabbi Dovid is not actually a *Rav,* a community rabbi, but when you want to show extreme honor to an individual, you do not always worry about minor details like that… "The wealthy Rabbi Dovid" is simply the description that I, on my own, chose to give him.

Reb Dovid was one of the original founders of our neighborhood, some thirty years ago. It seems that even back then, he had more money than others, which might explain why his house is built in the most beautiful location in the community. It sits on top of a hill overlooking the entire area.

How does Reb Dovid earn his money? What exactly is his business? Well, no one really knows, but the key word that seems to appeal to everyone is "import." Everyone knows that Reb Dovid deals with importing products and selling them. Simply put, he is an importer.

What exactly does he import? From what countries? To whom does he sell these imported products? It seems that most people, at least, have no answers. He always drives a brand new car, which he generally does not keep for more than a year or two; he then exchanges it for the latest model.

I remember a heated debate that once erupted in my class about Reb Dovid. Tall Elimelech, who always "knows everything," claimed that Reb Dovid imports electronic products. "Washing machines, dryers, vacuum cleaners, and things like that," he declared with absolute certainty.

Itzik, the class *chevreh'man*, on the other hand, passionately insisted that Reb Dovid imports cars. "Don't you see that he has a new car almost every year? Where do they all come from?" he asked us before immediately answering his own question – "He is the one who brings these cars into the country!"

"I'm telling you," burst in Yoki, who always liked to show off good "sources" for his arguments, "that Reb Dovid imports… air!"

"That's right," he continued, "nobody knows were he really gets his money from, but with my own ears I overheard my father telling my mother that Reb Dovid's whole 'import' business is, in his eyes, 'one big riddle.'" Those were Yoki's exact words.

Reb Dovid does not tell people how much he earns or other details like that. However, he does make a point of dropping hints about his wealth every now and again.

"A well known entrepreneur approached me this week," I heard Reb Dovid inform a group of men who had gathered around him outside the *mikveh*. "He suggested that I invest one hundred thousand dollars in a business that he believes will provide a return of three hundred percent in just two years. What can I tell you? I discussed it very seriously with him. I have heard that the business is extremely reliable. But with the global recession, I really don't think I want to take any extra risks. How can I know what will happen in just another month or two from now?"

Reb Dovid is a very imposing person. When he enters the *shul*, all eyes turn towards him almost automatically. Perhaps it has something to do the way that he walks, full of importance. Maybe it has to do with the fact that he speaks in an especially loud voice. Perhaps it's that his sons and sons-in-law surround him constantly, like a prime minister with his entourage. I do not quite know how to explain it, but his very presence seems to create "waves" all around him.

I never really properly investigated, but I get the feeling that not everyone in the community is sympathetic towards Reb Dovid. It is possible that some people are jealous of his wealth. Nevertheless, everyone without exception honors him.

Reb Dovid does not talk with just anyone. I would say that he has a close circle of friends and fans with whom he discusses his clever and fantastic accomplishments.

When I think deeply about all this, I realize that Reb Dovid is the exact opposite of another man in our community. His name is Ephraim.

Ephraim is around forty-five, a senior worker at the metal factory in Holon. He is a decent and polite man, who lives a quiet and modest life. Ephraim's two oldest sons are already studying in high school. All of his sons are serious and diligent students.

Financially, Ephraim is considered well-established. I once overheard Leizer the teacher informing Reb Shimon, who studies in the *Kolel* – although I have no idea why he was telling him this – that "Ephraim earns a good salary, *Boruch Hashem*." Despite that, Ephraim lives a modest lifestyle. He does not own his own car, and in our community, he drives around on a bike.

I never saw him compete for an honorable *aliyah* to the Torah in the *shul*, neither on *Shabbos* nor on any *Yom Tov*. While Reb Dovid and Reb Avraham (the owner of the only supermarket in our neighborhood) argue between themselves over the honor of reading *Maftir Yonah* or being called to the Torah for the *Aseres HaDibros*, Ephraim sits quietly in his place. Ephraim's seat is directly opposite ours, so I can clearly observe him. While the others debate honors, Ephraim gazes into a *Chumash* or some other *sefer*.

Personally, I am always much more impressed by modest people like Ephraim than those who make lots of noise and commotion. However, I reached the conclusion long ago that in communal life, things are not always judged according to their true worth. I know that many in our community respect and are very fond of Ephraim. Nevertheless, if you visit for even a short while, you will immediately notice which people determine and influence what goes on. Ephraim is certainly not one of them.

That is why it has always surprised me that Reb Dovid and Ephraim share a close and friendly relationship. True, Ephraim is not counted among the inner circle of friends who are always hanging around Reb Dovid, but the two of them do speak to each other often. They can be found in quiet discussion, just the two of them, in one of the further corners of the *shul*. It amazes me that two men who are so different from each other can find so much to talk about together.

The truth is that this is no longer an unresolved mystery. Just a few months ago, I discovered the answer in a most unpredictable way. Let me tell you, it was a most interesting revelation.

• • •

It happened one evening, after returning from school.

I am now in one of the higher grades, and next year, with Hashem's help, I will enter high school. When we finish our studies for the day, especially in the winter, it is already dark outside. I am lucky that my afternoon teacher this year is Rabbi Levin. He is an incredibly exciting teacher. No matter what subject we are studying, *Novi, Chumash,* or even *Halachah*, he always makes it exciting. If he was not so exciting, I greatly doubt that I would remain alert until the end of each day's studies. I sincerely hope that I get a teacher at least as interesting as Rabbi Levin when I enter high school, because they study until much later each day.

However, all that is not important right now.

That evening, when I went to lock my bike to the fence surrounding the steps in front of our apartment building, I discovered that another bike was there. I recognized it as belonging to Ephraim. I was very curious to know what had brought Ephraim to our building. I locked my bike to the opposite corner of the railing and quickly sprung up the steps to our home on the second floor.

I stepped inside and received another surprise. At that very moment, Ephraim was taking a seat on the armchair in the living room opposite my father. As I entered, my father looked up, waved hello to me, and then quickly turned his head back towards Ephraim. Perhaps I should note that my father and Ephraim are friends. True, they come from very different backgrounds and their businesses are extremely unlike each other – my father is a *sofer* – but there are similarities in their characters. Both my father and Ephraim are calm men, who live their lives at peace with those around them.

I slipped into my bedroom. One of its two doors faces the living room. That door was slightly open, and without even meaning to, I overheard the conversation between my father and Ephraim.

"I need your help," began Ephraim. "It is not actually me, but someone else in our community. The man has recently got himself into deep difficulties and needs a large bank loan to try and get back on his own two feet and begin again."

"So you want me to phone the bank and recommend that they allow him to take out such a loan?" asked my father with a smile.

"No," replied Ephraim, "What I have come for today will not even require you to pick up the phone."

Ephraim paused for a moment and then continued, "In order to receive this loan, he needs guarantors."

"Hmmm," my father answered in a cautious tone. "Exactly how large is this loan?"

"A quarter of a million shekel," Ephraim informed him.

"Oh my!" gasped my father in amazement, before adding, "If I am being asked to guarantee such a large sum, then I should

really know who is borrowing the money."

The living room became very still. I imagined Ephraim struggling to find the right words.

"Look, Reb Tzvi," he said at last, "I am certain that I can rely on you to keep this a complete secret. The main point is to help a fellow Jew, not to embarrass him. So…"

Ephraim again fell silent.

At last, he announced, "We are talking about… Reb Dovid."

"What?!" exclaimed my father in a half-cry. "What do you mean? He is…"

Ephraim cut him off before my father had a chance to finish the sentence.

"Correct. Until recently, he was a very successful businessman, and he continues to conduct himself in a way that indicates that nothing has changed. However, you should know that he it is now difficult for him to even cover the monthly expenses of his home."

I was completely shocked by what I overheard.

"He is an importer of luxurious bath accessories from Italy and the Far East," Ephraim explained. My heart skipped a beat. Finally, the mystery surrounding the nature of Reb Dovid's business has been solved.

"However, the current crisis in the construction industry seriously crippled him. In the past, Reb Dovid employed ten workers. Now he is struggling to keep just one – himself! He has tried to keep afloat for as long as possible in the hope that the global recession will improve."

"What – are – you – saying?" I heard my father exclaim, pronouncing each word slowly. Clearly, he was struggling to come to terms with the revelation.

"Exactly what you heard," replied Ephraim simply.

"What affects him more than anything else is the embarrassment. He does not reveal the true situation even to his closest friends. They still see him as the symbol of success. It is too hard for him to shatter the myth… Only I, and perhaps one other person – and now also you – know his well-kept secret."

"It's unbelievable," said my father. "We are really so dependent on Hashem!"

"But I want to tell you something else, Reb Tzvi," Ephraim continued. "Just as people mistakenly think that Reb Dovid is a rich man, when in fact he barely has a penny left to his name, they also do not know about his good heart and the acts of kindness he performs secretly without ever expecting a reward."

"Well, if you say so, then you must certainly know…" replied my father.

"Yes, I do know." Ephraim detected the tone of doubt in my father's voice.

"I know this because we are very close friends. I first grew close to Reb Dovid when he provided financial help to a family member who faced hardship. But I also know of other cases where Reb Dovid provided generous help. By the way, Alexander..."

Ephraim stopped in mid-sentence.

"What about him?" asked my father.

"Alexander," Ephraim repeated the name of the pauper who collected donations in the *shul*. "Who do you think looks after him? Makes sure his clothes are always clean? Gets him food to eat? That's right – it's Reb Dovid and his wife. Until today, they continue to care for his needs, even though they are struggling terribly themselves."

Well, what can I say? I sat in my room, not believing my ears. First, there was the astonishing discovery that Reb Dovid had lost his wealth. And then, the stories of Reb Dovid helping needy people secretly, including Alex the Beggar – I'm sorry, I mean Alexander Saltzman.

Just then, my mother called me from the kitchen. I had to go. I never had a chance to hear whether my father agreed to sign as a guarantor for the bank loan.

That was several months ago. I do not have any reliable information on the current financial situation of Reb Dovid. However, my inner feeling is that his situation has improved. Lately, he has also spent less time in private conversation with Ephraim.

The amazing thing about this whole story is that the people in our community have absolutely no idea what has been happening with Reb Dovid. Believe me, if people would know, I would have heard about it long ago from the boys in my grade.

As for me, I learned my lesson! Not to judge people just by what I see and assume to be the truth, without having any real knowledge.

A Moving Graduation Party

My parents and I have not yet decided which *yeshivah* I should attend in the coming year. Naturally, the decision is not only our own. The *yeshivah* will make the decision whether or not to accept me. In truth, I am not too worried about being accepted by any *yeshivah*, because I am considered one of the best students in my grade. Please excuse my "modesty" in saying so, but with you at least, I feel comfortable discussing these things openly...

We are debating between two *yeshivos*. The first is closer to our home, just a quarter of an hour's drive. The second is further, but is certainly a more impressive *yeshivah*.

It may interest you to know that my mother is the one who wants me to attend the more impressive *yeshivah*, while my father thinks I should be closer to home. He insists that he has not yet recovered from his own childhood trauma of being sent far away from home to study.

The reason that I am telling you all this is because this afternoon, for the first time, Rabbi Levin held a serious discussion with us about the need to prepare ourselves for entering *yeshivah*. He briefly described the daily schedule in *yeshivah* and made a few points that he felt were important for us to be aware of. Among other things, he mentioned the need to develop stamina and diligence in study, as well as the important role that social life plays in the *yeshivah* scene.

"*Yeshivah* means living with your friends twenty-four hours a day – studying together, eating together, and so on," Rabbi Levin explained. "To a great extent, your *yeshivah* friends become your 'family.'"

Truthfully, I feel that my grade has recently matured both academically and socially. Our classroom has become a strong learning environment. We have certainly had our fair share of fighting and rivalry for power and control in the past, but especially during the last few months, a sense of friendship and tolerance has prevailed.

Meni Feinberg joined us at the beginning of 6th grade, when his family moved into a nearby neighborhood. For the next two years, he remained a stranger in our class. It was not just that he had not grown up with us and therefore did not understand the way we saw things and our internal methods of operating. Rather, the main obstacle to Meni's fitting in was the fact that he never tried to do so. It seemed that fitting in simply did not concern him. We interpreted that as a sign of arrogance – that we were not worth his attention.

Meni had immigrated to Israel from the United States. He told us that even in America his parents had spoken to him in Hebrew. Nevertheless, he spoke Hebrew with a heavy American accent. Unfortunately, this became a reason to make fun of him. In particular, our class imitator Shuki would greatly enjoy imitating Meni's accent, and his unique sentences and expressions.

For example, instead of *anachnu* ("we"), Meni would say *anu*. Instead of *letzalem* ("to photograph"), he would say *lakachat temunah* (literally, "to take a picture"). And instead of *levade* ("to ascertain"), he would say *la'asot batu'ach* (literally, "to make sure"). Meni would make many other mistakes by literally translating English expressions and ideas into Hebrew.

Personally, I was divided in my approach to Meni. On the one hand, I did not like the fact that he kept himself distant from us. On the other hand, I greatly admired the fact that despite the teasing and joking at his expense, he always remained unintimidated – he never seemed to take our words to heart. For some boys, the fact that they could not upset Meni caused them to try even harder… I was also extremely impressed that Meni managed to remain polite and courteous. I never once saw him lose his cool.

I am naturally inclined to find a label for everyone and everything. I once thought deeply about Meni and tried my best to come up with a description for him. I finally reached the conclusion that he was, well, how should I put it? A little too… perhaps just a little too mature, too polite, too self confident, too normal. It might sound strange, but in the social life of our grade, it is sometimes difficult to handle someone who is a little too normal!

In seventh grade, the general attitude towards Meni began to turn hostile. What contributed greatly to this change was the fact that Meni flew to America a number of times during the year, each time for another reason. Once it was for the wedding of his cousin, another time it was "to be in the home of my grandfather and grandmother in upstate New York for *Pesach*." Yet a third time, it was to participate in the seventieth birthday celebration of his other grandfather in Springfield, Massachusetts. As if that was not enough, each time that he flew to America, he returned with new clothes and accessories, such as an expensive watch, a fancy fountain pen, and other luxuries.

No one can say that Meni was exactly guilty of breaking any laws, but the fact is that his flashy lifestyle made the other boys in the class thoroughly jealous. I also felt that all of his flights and expensive purchases were a little too showy.

The trouble was that the hostile attitude towards Meni affected all of us. His very presence in our class disturbed our general sense of harmony. Some boys constantly picked on him, others only from time to time, and yet others chose to completely ignore Meni and the commotion surrounding him. This caused debates and arguments between us.

Our teachers and the principal recognized the problem considerably late. For that reason, they found it difficult to improve the situation. The negative atmosphere that seemed to rule our classroom also damaged the quality of our studies.

Three weeks before the end of the school year, Meni flew to America for a fourth time. As far as the boys were concerned, this was more than enough. At first we thought, and even hoped, that he would not return. After two weeks, someone spread the rumor that the Feinberg family had left Israel for good and had moved back to America. We felt quite relieved.

Then, just three days before the end of the school year, Meni returned.

During that first recess, Meni surprised us by approaching each of us and handing out candy that he had brought back from America. That was a very pleasant gesture on his part. Throughout the rest of that day and the next, it seemed that the shell that had surrounded him had cracked slightly and that he was trying hard to befriend us.

The true drama, however, only occurred on the last day of our studies.

• • •

During the final session of the day, our 7th grade teacher Rabbi Katz, announced that our graduation party would be held that evening at the home of… Meni!

We were shocked.

Firstly, there had never been a graduation party at the end of any school year until now. Secondly, out of all places, he chose Meni's house! Meni did not even live in our neighborhood. Why was his home chosen?

"At six thirty sharp, straight after *maariv*, organized transportation will be leaving from outside the *shul*," Rabbi Katz announced. He then sent us home half an hour early, to give us time to prepare.

At the end of the *maariv*, we boarded the waiting bus. After a ten-minute journey, we arrived outside a detached house that was surrounded by a grassy lawn. A wooden mailbox shaped like a birdhouse held a small sign – "Feinberg Family."

At the door of the charming house, Meni and his father waited to greet us. "Welcome! *Beruchim haba'im!*" Meni's father, an impressive man, announced warmly.

"Thank you so much for coming!" added Meni with a slightly embarrassed smile, as he guided us towards the back porch of the house. There, a large table had been set with all sorts of goodies. As we passed the kitchen, I noticed Meni's mother looking at us. She seemed very pleased.

The event began with Rabbi Katz giving an overview of our past school year. He then asked who had prepared a *d'var Torah*, and a number of boys delivered interesting explanations of the weekly Torah portion. We sang a number of songs, and then our teacher declared, "You are certainly wondering why we have suddenly decided to hold a graduation party this year, and why we chose this location – in Meni's home."

These were exactly the questions that had been occupying our minds the entire time. We eagerly awaited his explanation. My mind raced with a few possible reasons, but I could never have imagined the actual cause.

"Therefore," Rabbi Katz continued, "the answer to these two questions will be answered by our dear host, Meni."

Meni coughed lightly.

"This party is a graduation party," he began, "the conclusion of a year of studies. But for me, this also marks a far more meaningful conclusion."

Well, it seems like Meni is about to leave our class, I thought to myself.

"This is my graduation party and also my thanksgiving party to personally thank Hashem," he informed us.

"You all know that I flew to America a number of times this year," Meni continued. "You were certain that I traveled for a number of different reasons, for happy family occasions. That's what I personally told you..."

I tried to understand why Meni felt it necessary to step on our toes right now, during our graduation party. What exactly was he attempting to accomplish?

Meni fell silent for a moment and then swallowed hard. It seemed that whatever he wanted to say was weighing heavily on his heart.

"I must apologize to you," Meni continued, and he lowered his eyes.

"Better late than never," whispered Shuki, who sat next to me at the table.

"I misled you," Meni announced. We all stared at him in surprise.

He then told us about a terrible blood disease that he had from the day he was born. Until recently, the disease was dormant and inactive. However, at the beginning of the past year, it suddenly became active and spread throughout his body. He was forced to travel repeatedly to America for expensive and painful treatments.

I was gripped with complete shock as I listened to his words. I looked around the table and saw that I was not the only one in shock.

"I did not want you to worry, so I did not share the true reason for my travels," Meni said simply. "While I was lying in hospital beds and receiving the treatments that greatly weakened me physically and also emotionally, I wondered whether I had done

the right thing. Maybe I should have told you so that you could all pray for me. That would have certainly helped me recover. But each time that a set of treatments were completed and I regained my strength, I again decided to stick to my original decision not to tell you. I just wanted to be treated like everyone else. I did not want you to pity me..."

At this point, I could no longer see my friends too well because I had lowered my eyes in deep, painful shame. How could we have allowed ourselves to be so critical and unpleasant to a classmate who was seriously ill and undergoing painful treatments, I asked myself. What else don't we know about the people that we interact with regularly, I wondered.

We listened in amazement as Meni continued his emotional words.

"When the treatments began, the doctors were unsure about the chances of success. But then, after the most recent treatments, the doctors reported that with Hashem's help they were successful in healing the disease."

Meni raised his eyes and surveyed us for a moment. If I was not mistaken, his eyes looked moist. Perhaps I was mistaken because my own eyes were wet with tears.

"I invited you all to my home tonight to tell you what I have been going through during the past year, so that I could hold a *se'udas hodoeh*, a thanksgiving ceremony together with you to thank Hashem that I recovered my health."

When Meni finished speaking, an oppressive silence surrounded the table. The heavy silence intensified our collective mood of complete embarrassment. How should we respond? What would be appropriate to say after hearing such words?

Rabbi Katz saved us by announcing in the name of the entire class our deep gratitude to Hashem for Meni's recovery. He wished Meni continued good health and then thanked Meni's father – who was standing at the side the entire time and watching with great emotion – for his warm hospitality and the enjoyable graduation party that he prepared for us all.

After the party, as we traveled back from Meni's home to our own neighborhood, we were finally able to speak freely and to analyze what had happened.

"I think we made a terrible mistake in our attitude to Meni," said Elimelech.

"I completely agree," responded Itzik.

"We were such idiots!" exclaimed Yoki and banged his head with both hands.

"Quite right," I added. "After all, it is much more pleasant to believe that we acted like that out of stupidity and not out of cruelty or spite..."

Those were rare moments of unanimous agreement in our grade. Even after much time had passed the effects of those moments were not lost. You can now appreciate why I mentioned earlier that the dramatic and moving story of Meni greatly increased the maturity level in our grade.

The Challenges of Wealth

There was a lot of fuss and commotion in our neighborhood last week. Why? Well, I think you will find the story behind all the tumult both strange and interesting.

First of all, I would like to provide some background information to give you a better general understanding:

Our neighborhood is not a rich one. The plots of agricultural land allocated to our neighborhood by the state are not especially large. Besides, agriculture has lost its appeal in recent years. The severe competition between the farmers, combined with other factors, has made it difficult to profit from agriculture.

It is a good thing that our neighborhood has two factories that provide jobs to many families and increase the tax funding provided to our community. One factory produces storage boxes, and the other factory, which belongs to "the tall Klein" (yes, there is also a "short Klein" in our community), produces yarns of high quality wool for knitting into clothes. The wool comes from sheep that are raised in Australia and England.

Despite this, there is still simply not enough income, and the neighborhood struggles with serious economic challenges on a daily basis.

How do I know this, you wonder? I explained earlier that I am somewhat of an investigator (or perhaps a little bit nosy)... Regardless, all this background information will allow you to appreciate the following scene.

Until today, some thirty years after our school was founded, it still does not have a designated room for *davening*. We are forced to *daven* in the lunchroom, creating much hassle and disorder. We also do not have our own Torah scroll or *aron kodesh* in which to place one. This forces us to transport a Torah scroll each Monday and Thursday from the *aron kodesh* of the *shul* across the road.

For years now, the community has been discussing the importance of a school *shul*; everyone is aware of the need to build one urgently. The school even has the grounds for a *shul* to be built. The only obstacle, not surprisingly, is a lack of funds.

Our school principal, Rabbi Shiyeh, is an extremely organized and responsible person. He repeatedly insists that he is not prepared to "drag the school's finances into a whirlpool of debt," as he put it. Rather, he declares, not a single brick will be laid for the school *shul* until he receives - in his own two hands - the funds to cover the entire cost of construction, from start to finish.

That is how things remained until a week ago. Then everything changed. What happened? Well, it became known that funds were indeed available for the entire construction.

So what was the problem? What caused all the commotion in the community?

That brings us – finally – to the actual story:

The problem was… please pay attention – that there was now too much money!

Oh, I see you are laughing. What sort of difficulty is that, you ask? Can't we use the extra money to build an even bigger and fancier *shul*? Or use it for another important purpose?

Apart from that, you must be wondering with surprise, how did the school suddenly go from not having any money at all, to having too much?

It all started a month ago.

Reb Avraham, the owner of the supermarket, entered the office of Rabbi Shiyeh. He informed the principal that in honor of the upcoming first *yahrtzeit* of his (Reb Avraham's) father, Reb Berel, he is interested in financing all the expenses required for the construction of a school *shul*. The *shul* would then bear his late father's name and memory.

One of the teachers who was present at the time later repeated the precise details of that meeting. At first, Rabbi Shiyeh was completely taken by surprise. He then blurted out in amazement, "Do you know what sort of sum we are talking about? It's over a million shekel!"

Reb Avraham was not fazed by the amount. "That is more or less what I had estimated," he explained, "And with Hashem's help, I will provide those funds. My father deserves a place of eternal honor in our community, and I am prepared to do whatever is necessary to make it happen, even if it means digging into a number of savings in the bank."

It is important to note that Rabbi Berel Lipner, the father of Reb Avraham, was one of the founders of our community. He was also the first teacher in the school, which was opened just days after the first families moved into their homes. It made a lot of sense to build a *shul* in his name at the school in which he served as the original teacher. That his own son came up with the idea and was also willing to personally fund the *shul* was perfectly natural and appropriate.

Rabbi Shiyeh replied to Reb Avraham's proposal with warm and heartfelt words.

"I have no words to thank you, Reb Avraham," he said with emotion. "The magnitude of the merit that you have generated in heaven through your generosity on behalf of the schoolchildren – whom our *chachomim* describe as "breath untainted by sin" – is impossible to imagine.

"It is simply unbelievable – how things are able to suddenly fall into place in such an amazing way and without any prior indication. Clearly, the kindness of Hashem…!"

Reb Avraham lightly nodded his head. It was clear that he was completely at peace with his decision to undertake such an expensive project.

All of a sudden, Rabbi Shiyeh's face became extremely serious. He looked like he had just seen a ghost.

"There is just one slight problem that I am sure we will be able to resolve," he said quickly.

"A problem?!" asked Reb Avraham in amazement. "What sort of problem could there be already?"

"Well… the problem is..." Rabbi Shiyeh began haltingly with a sheepish smile on his face. "Not that it is really correct to call it a 'problem,' but… you know, Reb Avraham, that there is such a thing as 'challenges of wealth'..."

"What are you referring to?" demanded Reb Avraham impatiently.

Rabbi Shiyeh struggled to find the right words.

"I am referring to the fact that just two days ago, someone else showed up here at my office, someone else from our community… and you are not going to believe this… he had a very similar proposal to yours..."

Reb Avraham swallowed hard. His face went white for a moment.

"What on earth do you mean…? What are you talking about…? Perhaps you won't mind explaining yourself…?"

Rabbi Shiyeh pressed himself forward. He placed his hand sympathetically on Reb Avraham's arm.

"What happened is that just two days ago, as I told you, someone sat in the exact chair that you are now sitting in. It was Ephraim.

He offered to finance the construction of a school *shul* in the memory of his late mother who had passed away tragically at a young age, leaving a young husband and three young orphans..."

"Ephraim?! Ephraim Peshititzky?!" Reb Avraham thundered in surprise. "With all due respect to him – is he even able to accept the financial burden of a million shekel construction project?"

"I also asked him that question," replied Rabbi Shiyeh in a soft, appeasing tone. "He told me that he is not planning to do it alone. He has a brother in France and another brother in South Africa. Both of them are successful businessmen, so he tells me. Together, they intend to share the expenses of building a *shul* for our school."

Reb Avraham gave the principal a piercing glare. It is difficult to know exactly what thoughts were racing through his mind at that moment.

• • •

Rabbi Shiyeh appeared somewhat embarrassed.

"Well, who would have believed it?" he muttered to himself. "For decades we had no money at all for the school *shul*. And then, all of a sudden we have *two* donors offering the full amount at the same time, each wanting to build the *shul* in memory of their parent!

"But you know what..." Rabbi Shiyeh attempted to convey a sense of control over the situation, "we are certainly not short of good ideas in terms of construction projects for new developments in our school. For example, I have been dreaming for years about opening an educational reading library that will be truly worthy of its name. In addition, the playing field desperately needs upgrading..."

Reb Avraham rose from his seat in anger.

"A *shul!* That is the only thing for which I am prepared or interested in donating such a substantial sum of money – not for anything else!"

He fell silent for a moment and then added, "By the way, I am not ready to give up on this project… with all due respect to Ephraim Peshititzky and his two brothers from the Diaspora, it seems to me that my father has the first right by far to a place of honor in this school..."

The news quickly spread throughout the community. Everyone seemed to be talking about the most unusual "conflict" between Reb Avraham and Ephraim. Since then, people have been heatedly debating who deserves the right to build the *shul* in our school. Within a few days, the neighborhood divided itself into the Camp of Avraham and the Camp of Ephraim. Don't worry, the debates have not turned into fights, *Boruch Hashem.*

I would like to draw your attention to an interesting observation. Most of the elderly residents support Reb Avraham, whose father was one of the original founders of the community, as we have mentioned. The less-elderly residents side with Ephraim. Is it possible that the debate will be decided, not according to the actual validity of the claims, but rather, according to the people making them?

Anyway, it was clear that this issue would have to be resolved by a *Rav.*

"We can rely on Rabbi Eleh," I overheard Yossel the *Gabbai* tell the "wealthy" Reb Dovid. "The *Rav* has proven quite capable of working his way out of confusing tangles."

"Personally, I have no doubt that he will decide in favor of Ephraim," replied Reb Dovid while running his hand over his tie. "It is completely obvious that he is right."

In this case, Reb Dovid made an exception in that he disagreed with the opinion of the elder members of our community. The truth is that after all that I discovered about the close friendship between Reb Dovid and Ephraim, I am not too surprised.

By the way, if it interests you, I was also inclined to support Ephraim in this case. What is *your* opinion on this whole debate?

As it turned out, at the end of a stormy week, Reb Avraham and Ephraim met in the office of the *Rav*. Most of us were certain that sparks would fly at that meeting and one of the parties would leave angry and bitter. That did not happen. Instead, to everyone's great surprise, after just a short while *both* parties exited the room of the *Rav* with beaming faces.

Much later, we found out – directly from one of the parties – precisely what had taken place in that meeting.

"Firstly," began the *Rav*, "I must express my great pride and emotion.

"You see, in all the years that I had been a *Rav*, I have never encountered a case such as this, where the two parties are fighting for the privilege to donate a large sum of money!"

The *Rav* then explained the importance of peace.

"Our *chachomim* teach us that 'the Torah was given just for the sake of making peace in the world.' They also said that 'Hashem's presence comes only where there is joy.' It is therefore impossible that a place designated for Hashem to rest His presence, a place whose purpose is to advance the Torah, should be built with argument and strife."

The *Rav* then turned to each of the parties and asked them to explain their position. He also asked them exactly when and how the idea of donating the *shul* in memory of their parents entered their minds.

Ephraim was asked to speak first.

"When my mother, of blessed memory, died, she was a very young woman," he described with deep feeling. "When she left us, all joy departed our home. We were left alone – a heartbroken father and three young orphans, the eldest being just thirteen years of age."

Ephraim swallowed hard and then concluded with a bitter smile, "When I say that all joy – *simchah* – was lost from our house, I also refer to the fact that my mother's name was Simchah..."

As he spoke, the *Rav* continued to gaze at Ephraim and listen attentively to his narrative, but it was clear that something else was also racing through his mind.

When Ephraim finished presenting his claims, Reb Avraham began to speak.

He did not need to say too much. Everyone in the community was familiar with his father, Reb Berel Lipner. Nevertheless, Reb Avraham described in glowing terms the famous first teacher in our community's school.

"There is no question that in all matters related to the school, my father deserves to receive preference," he concluded his speech firmly.

Then it was the *Rav*'s turn to summarize the arguments.

"As I said earlier," he began in his deep, soothing voice, "It is not possible to build the new *shul* in a state of argument and upset. It must be built with peace and joy shared by all the members of our community.

"I have listened to both of you carefully and have found each of your arguments strong. The solution, however, is to build the *shul* together. You can then make it larger and more attractive, with an expensive *aron kodesh* to house the Torah scrolls, which you can have made to the highest degree of perfection, and so on."

The *Rav* paused for a moment and then continued, "The only problem, as we are well aware, is the naming. After whose parent shall we name the *shul*?"

Again, the *Rav* fell momentarily silent. He suddenly turned to Reb Avraham.

"If I am not mistaken, if my memory serves me correctly… Berel was not your father's only name, correct?"

"That's right," replied Reb Avraham, "his full name was Berel Simchah and that was a most fitting name, actually, because he was always happy."

The *Rav*'s eyes flew wide open and seemed to sparkle with sudden insight.

"Wonderful! Marvelous! But that's just great!" he exclaimed with great emotion. "If so, then we have also solved the naming of the *shul*!"

Ephraim and Reb Avraham stared at the *Rav* in astonishment. What did he mean? Why did he seem so delighted?

"What don't you understand?" replied the *Rav* to their stares. "The new *shul* that you will jointly build will be named *Beis Simchah!* That way, it will be named for your mother, Reb Ephraim, and also for your father, Reb Avraham. True, your father was known by his first name, but certainly for the sake of peace he would willingly forgo a fraction of his honor and be pleased to have the new *shul* carry his second name."

That, then, was the creative solution of the *Rav* that brought a most pleasant conclusion to the stormy debate raging in our community. His solution also served to remind us all just why we all enjoy and respect our *Rav* so very much.

Horsetail Knotweed

Every Thursday, our grade is tested on the *Gemara* we have learned over the course of the past week. Rabbi Shimon, one of the young men studying in the *Kolel* in our *yeshivah*, is in charge of the testing. He is an extremely lively kind of person. As soon as he enters our room, the entire class is fired with enthusiasm. His energetic character perfectly matches the ginger color of his beard and his alert green eyes that seem to constantly sparkle. We call him "The Tester."

Rabbi Shimon is a Torah scholar and a very smart man. It is extremely difficult to trick him. For example, when a student who is not up to standard repeats the words of *Rashi* or *Tosefos* without actually understanding what he is reading, Rabbi Shimon immediately senses it. He also makes certain – cleverly and gently – that the student is aware that he (Rabbi Shimon) knows that the student does not know his material.

On the other hand, when a student is fluent in the subject but is confused by his own nervousness when answering a question, Rabbi Shimon senses that as well. In such cases, he calms the student and gives him a second opportunity to prove that he truly knows his material.

For that reason, we all admire and respect Rabbi Shimon. After all, as I realized long ago, we boys appreciate adults who combine tenderness with authority and who are difficult to trick (even if that sometimes works out "worse" for us…).

To a great extent, you could say that Rabbi Shimon is one of the reasons the boys in our grade put great effort into arriving well prepared for the test. Each Wednesday evening, you can find boys from our grade in the *shul*, learning in pairs, perfecting their knowledge and sharpening their understanding of the material – all because of the next morning's test.

There are twenty-three boys in our class. We can be divided almost equally into three. One third are excellent, another third are average, and the remainder are weak. These descriptions refer only to mental abilities, not to the outcome. In actuality, almost the entire class achieves well. Almost the entire class. To be exact, the entire class except for one student who, in order not to disclose his identity, we will call him Chaim.

Chaim is a dreamer. In case you misunderstand me, let me clarify that Chaim is in no way unintelligent. Exactly the opposite – he contains an entire encyclopedia in his head. He is knowledgeable in almost every subject, and especially in anything connected to botany and zoology, the study of plants and animals. He can explain everything related to the ant kingdom that crawls beneath and on the surface of the ground. He knows the precise name of any bird perched on a branch or soaring through the sky. He recognizes plants whose names sound like they are taken from science fiction.

For example, have you ever heard of Horsetail Knotweed? I know you haven't! How about Emarginated Mullein? Or Bryonia Cretica? Well, if you happen to accompany Chaim on one of his journeys to the slopes at the west of our neighborhood, you will search – just as I searched – for some of these strange-sounding plants.

We used to call him "the scientist," but as the years went by this changed to "the dreamer"...

It sometimes takes Chaim more than an hour for his morning walk to school; he is hardly ever on time to class. His home is at the edge of our neighborhood, although his family did not always live there – but that is another story altogether, which we will eventually get to.

Chaim finds it necessary to examine each petal and leaf, to stand still and think about each bird or butterfly, and to closely check each ant that drags a crumb of food into its hole.

Chaim is certainly a walking encyclopedia.

Nevertheless, he is completely tuned out of whatever we happen to be learning in class. At the beginning of the year, it seemed as though Chaim was making an effort to control himself and follow the studies. This is *yeshivah*, after all... However, right after the *Yomim Tovim*, he slipped back into his world of insects, plants and dreams.

He sat in the classroom, but he was not really there. He stared at the teacher, but did not listen in the slightest to what he was

actually saying. When a fly entered the classroom, something that disturbed us, Chaim was as delighted as can be. He began tracing the flight path of the fly, concentrating on the rapid fluctuation of its wings, noticing the way it rubbed its front legs against each other, and other things about which I have no knowledge.

That was Chaim at his best.

He was not always like that, though. I still remember what most of my friends perhaps try to forget: that until two years ago, Chaim was a regular student like the rest of us. Perhaps he was not exactly the most studious boy in the grade, but neither was he an exceptionally weak student. Then, something suddenly happened to him. He began to float through the classes without paying attention. In professional language, if I am not mistaken, that is described as an "attention and concentration disorder."

Rabbi Shimon the Tester follows Chaim's condition with great interest. He shows him an admirable amount of patience. I paid attention to the fact that he first asks him easy questions, despite his telling Chaim repeatedly that he is capable of much more.

"You are a smart boy," he once told Chaim during a test in front of the whole class, causing him to turn as red as a tomato. "You are extremely intelligent. There is no reason why you should not know the *Gemara* with all the commentary of *Rashi* and *Tosefos* backwards and forwards!"

From all the expressions used by Rabbi Shimon, I realized that there was some kind of blockage in Chaim's life, an external cause that did not allow him to concentrate during classes. Rabbi Shimon asked him a number of times how he was able to retain such vast knowledge of nature and science, while he found it difficult to understand even a simple section of *Gemara*. Chaim, however, was simply unable, or perhaps he was just unwilling, to offer a logical answer to this riddle.

"I find it hard to concentrate," he would always answer.

During this week's test, something surprising happened. Perhaps we could even say it was completely unprecedented.

Rabbi Shimon asked Chaim a simple question. The answer was clearly spelled out in black and white on the page of *Gemara* open in front of Chaim. However, Chaim simply shrugged his shoulders in confusion. Rabbi Shimon then fell silent for a few moments and was clearly deep in thought.

"I would like to share something with you," he broke the silence. We all grew as tense as coiled springs.

"This is a personal story that I have not told publicly until today, and certainly not to children of your age. However, I think that the moral of the story is very important and you will surely benefit from it. For that reason, I am prepared to reveal something about myself that will surprise you..."

• • •

"If I would ask you to guess where I was born, I am positive that you would choose the name of a city or settlement that is frum," Rabbi Shimon continued while he gazed at the entire class, from side to side. "That is because you assume that I was raised and educated in a home that observed and studied the Torah. You would assume that since I was an infant, my parents taught me Torah and educated me with a deep respect for Hashem."

He paused for a moment, ran his fingers through his ginger beard, and prevented a light laugh from escaping his lips.

"Is that not correct?" he asked us, blinking two or three times.

I nodded and from the corners of my eyes, I noticed other heads nodding in agreement.

"The truth, however, is completely different. In fact, I was born in the heart of Tel Aviv, to a family that was alienated from Torah and *mitzvos*. My father was a doctor of literature and my mother was, and still is, an expert consultant for natural nutrition. In the home in which I spent most of my childhood, the topics discussed involved books and authors that lacked any Jewish connection. It was all about health and nature."

I was stunned. Rabbi Shimon?! The young man studying diligently in *Kolel?* Our sharp minded Tester? We were all shocked.

"Yes, yes, exactly as you heard," Rabbi Shimon answered, reading our thoughts. "My father never took me to *shul*, not even on *Rosh Hashanah* or *Yom Kippur*. I would not care to tell you the menu at our table on *Pesach*. This was not done out of defiance or anything like that. It was just that my parents were raised with complete alienation from any spark of Torah and *mitzvos*."

The Tester coughed lightly before continuing.

"There was a religious school not far from our home. I did not know at the time that such a school is called a *cheder*. This *cheder* was located just two streets away from the school at which I studied, so that I was forced to pass it twice a day, each morning and evening.

"The students on the other side of the fence appeared to me strange and even ridiculous. They always wore long, dark pants with closed shoes or black sandals. They wore strange velvet *yarmulkas* with two *payes* dangling from either side of them. To tell you the truth, I had great pity on them and at the same time, I despised them. To me, they looked like aliens from another planet. A number of times, I made offensive comments as I passed by. They did not restrain themselves from responding, although they labeled me with terms that I did not even understand. I could see that they also looked at me as if I had come from another planet.

"At some point, I realized that we were truly from two different worlds and that we did not share a common language. I then stopped making fun of them. I told myself that it is extremely childish to laugh and ridicule someone with whom you are completely unfamiliar and whose lifestyle you do not recognize.

"In seventh grade, when I was around twelve years old, I began to grow curious about them. As I passed them, I would deliberately slow down and carefully observe them. I noticed them playing games, some of which I recognized. There was something pleasant and refined about their faces and movements. They ran and spoke energetically, but without any aggression. They never used curse words or foul language. I hardly ever saw them fighting physically. This was extremely different from my own school scene.

"I suddenly felt a deep longing to understand their "codes" and to discover something more about their world. What makes them happy? What makes them sad? More importantly, what are their goals in life?

"One day, something clicked – I felt myself envying them. They seemed far calmer than my friends and I, more at peace with

themselves, and happier. I remember that once on my way back from school with two friends, we came across a group of these religious students more or less the same age as us, standing in a circle and… singing! They were like a kind of choir, singing a stirring song in an accent that I did not recognize. At first we just stood there, my two friends and I, staring at them in enchantment. Then one of my friends wanted to pick up a rock and throw it at them to scare them and break up the group. But I stopped him. My two friends carried on walking home, while I remained rooted to my place. I listened as they sang and felt my heart melting.

"Thoughts about those strange boys on the other side of the fence did not let me rest. They occupied my mind even while I tried to fall asleep at night. I would wait impatiently for the moments each day in which I would again pass by the *cheder* and watch the boys at play, walking around or singing. I wanted to get to know them.

"A number of times, I wanted to discuss my thoughts and feelings with my parents, but I held myself back. I felt that they would think I had gone crazy. Nevertheless, I once told my father about the *chareidi* boys that I see each day.

"'I do not understand anything about them,' he replied, 'even though my grandfather was devoutly religious. That was a very long time ago – and it was in the Diaspora...'"

Rabbi Shimon glanced at his watch. He then drew a deep breath (it seemed to me that he also gave a silent sigh) and quickly continued his story.

"One sunny morning, my entire life changed. During the first recess, I was called home from school. One of my family members was waiting for me there and he told me that my father had suffered a serious heart attack and was hospitalized at the Ichilov Hospital.

"We traveled together to the hospital. I was not allowed to approach my father, who lay in a hospital bed anesthetized and attached to a breathing machine. I watched him through the large glass windows of the Intensive Care Unit. To my great sadness and grief, he did not survive even another twenty-four hours. The next morning, we accompanied his coffin to the cemetery. This was a wound that was irreparable. In one moment, my mother and I lost what was most precious to us than anything else."

We listened to Rabbi Shimon's unbelievable story as if we had been hypnotized. I stole a glance at Chaim. Just for once, he was listening with absolute concentration.

"During the seven days of mourning, a man with a distinguished-looking face entered our home. He had an elegant beard and a round black hat. I seemed to recognize him from somewhere. He sat quietly for a few minutes and then asked permission to say a few words of Torah. He spoke about the eternality of the soul and how a person's life does not end when his soul departs his physical body. He added that the *neshamah* of the departed continues to watch over the people to whom he was close during his life in this world, and that the departed hopes that his dear ones will do something for the elevation of his *neshamah* in the world of truth - *olam ho'emes*.

"My mother and I, and all those present, listened to his words with great respect. 'And how exactly are we able to do something for Dani?' my mother suddenly asked. Dani was my father's name. The man gave me a strong look and then said in a soft tone, 'For example, if this charming young boy would recite the *kaddish....*'

"That is how I first came to know my teacher, Rabbi Azriel Valles, the senior principal of the *cheder* Emunah VaDaas in Tel Aviv. He lived in the building closest to our home, although I only discovered all these details much later..."

• • •

"My connection with Rabbi Azriel grew stronger all the time. To begin with, I used to meet him at the *shul* after *minchah* and *maariv*, following which I would recite *kaddish*. After some time, he taught me sections of *davening*. A while later, I began to arrive for *shachris* as well. I then asked, and my mother gave her permission, for Rabbi Azriel to teach me Torah. We would sit together between *minchah* and *maariv* and we would learn *Chumash*, *Mishneh*, and some of the *Halachas* from *Kitzur Shulchan Aruch*. I found my heart drawn to the new worlds that were suddenly revealed to me.

"My mother watched the change that had come over me with some anxiety, but as time passed, her anxiety lessened. I would share with her the information that I had learned with Rabbi Azriel and it impressed her. My mother had always been a spiritual kind of person and that spiritual side now found a way to express itself in actuality. Within a few months, our house looked completely different. We fixed *mezuzos* to every doorpost and a friendly Rabbi came to make our kitchen kosher. My mother purchased a number of books on the basics of *yiddishkeit*, and began to personally participate in Torah classes.

"The inner change that I experienced also had external results. I began wearing a *yarmulka* on my head. *Tzitzis* dangled at the sides of my pants. You may be amazed, but my friends did not bother me over these changes. They seemed to think that I was doing all this as an expression of mourning for my father.

"One day, I discovered that Rabbi Azriel was in fact the principal of the *cheder* near my home. I told him that I had been passing by his school for years. Naturally, I also told him about the thoughts that went through my mind at seeing the students – long before my father passed away and long before I knew Rabbi Azriel. He smiled broadly when he heard all this, and said, 'Well, now you are finally able to check out the school from the inside of the fence as well.' I jumped happily at the opportunity. The next day, I accompanied Rabbi Azriel to his office. From then on, I stopped in at his office each day on my way home from school and exchanged a few words.

"On my first visits, the students crowded around and stared at me as if I was a suspicious package. But after a short while they grew accustomed to seeing me there. Soon enough, I developed a friendship with some of the students.

"I won't tire you with all the small details, but in the end, after Rabbi Azriel held many convincing talks with my mother, I found myself one morning studying in the *Cheder* Emunah VaDaas.

"Do you think that my journey to *yiddishkeit* stopped there?" Rabbi Shimon interrupted his narrative. He again checked his watch and looked surprised. "Just a moment," he said, "It is already time for recess. With Hashem's help I will continue, next week."

"Please continue! Please continue!" came the desperate cry from everyone in the classroom. "We would gladly skip recess for the rest of the story!"

Rabbi Shimon beamed.

"I did not know that the story was that exciting," he added with a wink. He seemed to be smiling within himself. After a moment he announced, "Okay, I will make it short and get to the main point...

"In truth, this was only the beginning of my journey. It was not an easy journey for a child who knew nothing about the basics of the *Mishneh, Gemara, Halachah,* and Jewish outlook. I did not really know anything at all!

"It was also a difficult journey because of my friends. My peers from my previous school could not understand what had happened to their friend all of a sudden. They demanded answers that I could not exactly provide. My distancing from them and connecting with the new group of friends took great inner strength from me. Then there were also difficulties in learning. I was in eighth grade, when the students normally prepare for entry into *yeshivah*. My level of knowledge was lower than a first grade student in *cheder*...

"As I said earlier, I will keep this short. The bottom line is that within a year or two of heroic struggling and great effort I managed to make up for all that I had missed from the earlier grades. By the time I was in *shiur gimmel* of *Yeshivah Ketanah,* no one would have realized that I was not raised in a religious home. In *Yeshivah Gedolah*, I made it, with Hashem's help, to the group of top students of the *yeshivah*."

Rabbi Shimon rose from his seat and began walking up and down the classroom.

"Well?" he suddenly demanded. "Would you have ever imagined all that?"

"No way!" We answered.

"So what do you have to say about it now? Is it possible to overcome obstacles? Is it possible to succeed if you truly want to?"

We answered all together in a babble of voices and replies. "Yes!" "I guess so..." "Certainly!"

Rabbi Shimon returned to his seat. He now fixed a sympathetic look at Chaim, who still appeared to be under the powerful spell of the discovery of Rabbi Shimon's personal story.

"I spoke to everyone in the class," said Rabbi Shimon, "but my main intention was to speak to you. There is still another seven months until the end of the school year and your entry into *yeshivah*. You can still progress with great success and with Hashem's help, enter *yeshivah* well prepared. It depends only on your decision. If you want to – you can."

For a few moments, Chaim looked at Rabbi Shimon with a serious and thoughtful expression on his face. His eyes seemed to say, "Okay."

"I am certain," Rabbi Shimon added, looking around the room, "that there are good students among you who would be happy to lend a hand to Chaim."

I do not know why, but it seemed to me that he fixed his eyes for a short while – on me!

The Tester closed his *Gemara*, then rose and left the room. The first few minutes were filled with a storm of talk and noise. Even the tall Elimelech who always "knows everything" openly admitted that he did not have the slightest idea of all that Rabbi Shimon told us. We were very touched by the fact that the Tester trusted us with his confidence, revealing his amazing personal story to us.

As things turned out, I found myself walking beside Chaim on the way home. I live right near the supermarket of Reb Avraham that is located in the very center of our neighborhood. Chaim, on the other hand, lives on the very edge of the community.

"Would you like to come to my house tonight?" Chaim asked me suddenly.

I was amazed at the invitation. Ever since his family moved to the outskirts of the neighborhood, Chaim had stopped inviting his friends to his home.

"Why not?" I replied.

To tell the truth, I did not really like the idea, but I decided that I had better not ruin such a rare invitation. If Chaim had finally decided to open up a little bit and reach out to someone, I certainly did not want to be the one to push him away.

"Very good," said Chaim with a great smile on his face. We made up to meet at nine o'clock.

"I am inviting you," Chaim added in an apologetic tone, "because there is something that I want to tell you."

• • •

Chaim's home is fairly small, but organized and clean. There are three siblings – an older sister, Chaim, and a younger brother. My visit lasted about one hour, but the thoughts that I was left with have not left me even today. Wait a minute, I haven't told you what happened...

Chaim opened the door for me and brought me straight into his bedroom. On the way, I managed to see his father and younger brother playing on the carpet in the living room with a giant plastic ball. Chaim's father held the child and helped him slowly and carefully roll the ball.

Chaim's room surprised me. I thought that it would look like the office of an absentminded professor, but it was in perfect order. There was a bed and a desk with shelves above it that were loaded with books. Some were *seforim*, others reading material. Among them were quite a few books on plant and animal life. That, at least, was something that I completely expected.

"So this is your small kingdom," I said to break the ice.

"You could say so," smiled Chaim. He suggested that I sit on the office chair beside the desk, while he went to the kitchen to fetch "a few good things." Meanwhile, I had a few moments to carefully examine the room.

On the wall, there was a family portrait apparently taken during a trip. In the picture, Chaim's sister appeared a year or two older than him. She was walking – or more like jumping – while holding her mother's hand. They both appeared happy and smiling. On the other hand, Chaim's father – despite experiencing a precious family moment – appeared somewhat bothered. He was holding the hand of the youngest child, a sweet little boy with two large dark eyes and wild curly hair. Chaim did not appear in the picture at all.

"Why are you not in the picture?" I asked him as soon as he entered the room holding a tray with a plate filled with wafers and two cups of freshly squeezed orange juice at its side.

"Who do you think took the picture?" Chaim replied.

"You're right," I laughed. "I don't know why I did not think of that!"

"Your younger brother is so cute," I said, throwing another look at the portrait on the wall. "What's his name?"

Chaim gave me a thoughtful stare. "We call him Mordechai. Or Motty for short. But in the house, we call him Motek."

While Chaim spoke about his brother, his eyes sparkled in a way that told me that he truly loved his younger brother. Nevertheless, he did not smile at all while he answered.

Chaim seemed a little hesitant. He set the tray down on the desk and said, "Come. Come and I'll show you something."

We went out of the room and walked along the porch to the back door of the living room. He stood with me at his side. "Look!" he said, and nodded with his head in the direction of his younger sibling who was sitting on one of the corners of the carpet. The giant ball rested not far from him. He was holding a slipper in his hand and looking at it. No, he was staring intensely at it. His head was covered with a large *yarmulka* that was fastened onto his wild hair with clips. Now that I was observing him from up close, I noticed something strange about him.

"He can sit like that for hours," whispered Chaim.

"What do you mean?" I asked, trying to understand what he was getting at.

"I mean that he is not an ordinary child," Chaim answered, throwing me a mature look. "He lives in a bubble. He has his own world, and no one has been able to penetrate it. He seems unaware to whatever is happening around him."

"Are you trying to tell me that your brother is…" I hesitated to use the term… "autistic?"

Chaim tilted his head slightly to one side and nodded. "Yes," he replied, "Motek is autistic. Exactly that."

I tried to mask my shock. I had once heard briefly about autism, but knew nothing beyond that. I also did not know whether Chaim was comfortable with me asking any further questions about the subject.

Chaim's mother glanced over to the window. "Oh, you are here? Father just left to a class and I need to speak on the phone. Do you mind keeping an eye on Motek for a few minutes?"

"Okay," answered Chaim, without any hesitation.

"He has to be watched the entire time," he explained to me.

"Why?" I asked in surprise, "You told me that he could sit for hours without moving!"

"That's right," Chaim responded, "but in one second the entire situation could change drastically. He sometimes goes into a fit of rage and it is difficult to restrain him. He could break everything in his way and even hurt himself. He could bang his head against the wall until it bleeds."

That sounded extremely disturbing to me.

"How old is he?" I asked with a mixture of alarm and interest. "Four," he replied.

I continued to observe Chaim for a minute or two. Then Chaim's mother returned and we were free to return to the bedroom. I sat on the chair and Chaim sat on his bed. He asked me if I wanted some wafers and handed me a cup of juice.

"Basically, I invited you here because of him," Chaim announced all of a sudden.

When he saw that I did not understand, he explained himself, "Because of Motek, I mean. I wanted you to see him. And I wanted to talk to you about him."

I was puzzled, "Why do you find it so important that I know about Motek?" As I said the name "Motek" I felt a little closer to Chaim.

He thought for a few moments.

"Because my decline in studies began about two years ago, when we first discovered that Motek was autistic. Our entire life changed. The whole house began to revolve around him. My parents even sold our old home just to have enough money to look after Motek."

He fell silent again.

"I also feel that my parents are embarrassed because of Motek's condition. As if they were somehow responsible for the fact that he was born autistic. For that reason, they almost never take him out of the house."

"And all this has a negative affect on your studies," I concluded.

"Yes," answered Chaim. "Especially the sense of secrecy surrounding Motek and his condition. This, I think, is what weighs me down the most."

Chaim seemed to be choosing his next words carefully.

"That's it," he finally declared. "I am determined to help my parents break through their wall of embarrassment. I am convinced that if everyone would be aware of Motek's condition, it would be a lot easier for all of us."

"And I have been chosen as the first person to whom you revealed this secret, and also the person to help spread this information to others?" I attempted to understand.

"Exactly!" responded Chaim. "You will certainly know how to explain my situation to our classmates in a clever and sensitive way. When they become aware, they will share the information with others."

• • •

I returned home and without realizing, my feet carried me to the bedside of my younger brother Dudi. It was now just before ten at night and he was already sleeping deeply. I carefully stretched out my hand towards him and gently stroked his angelic face with great love. I looked at the small *yarmulka* on his head and spent a few moments in thought.

People just do not know how much they ought to thank Hashem for every second of health and livelihood, I thought to myself. I then realized that I had heard my parents say the same thing a number of times. Now, at least, I felt that I actually understood what they meant.

Dudi, who turned four a month ago, yawned in his sleep and rolled on top of the blanket that had been covering him.

Wow! A forgotten memory suddenly surfaced. I just remembered that Dudi and Chaim's brother Motek were born only days apart. How could I have forgotten that? I wondered at myself. How could I not have remembered the joint notice that was posted on the new bulletin board in our classroom announcing *"Mazal tov* on the birth of the new brothers!" That notice had mentioned both of our names.

My heart ached. It was clear that while we merited a healthy child, *Boruch Hashem*, and we greatly enjoyed his wonderful development from day to day – along with his clever tricks and the smart things he already manages to say – Chaim's family had to cope with a heartbreaking condition.

I fell asleep very late that night. Thoughts of Chaim and his family did not leave my mind. I imagined Motek staring silently at his slipper and then suddenly springing to his feet and going on a rampage of destruction through the house. After that, I imagined Chaim suggesting that he take Motek to the park, and his mother telling him, "You go by yourself, Chaim. I'll look after Motek in the house..."

The next day, Chaim seemed to be concentrating better during class. Perhaps the fact that he shared his painful secret with me made it a bit easier for him.

I did not tell all my classmates about my visit to Chaim's home and his secret that he had shared with me. I first told Itzik and Nachum, my best friends. Then Meni and Yoki. Meni really took the story to heart. "How terrible!" he mumbled to himself, "such suffering!" I had always thought that Meni was more mature and unique than the rest of the grade – and if you remember what happened at the end of the previous school year, you will appreciate how my conclusion was greatly strengthened by the news of his own medical condition.

I then asked these four classmates to leak the news to the others.

Two days later, Chaim went home early, during the first recess. This was the perfect opportunity to hold an open class discussion about Motek.

"Firstly," declared Elimelech with authority, "We need to find a way to inform Chaim that we are all aware of his brother's condition and that he no longer needs to act as if it were a guarded secret."

I am generally not too excited about Elimelech's authoritarian way of speaking, but this time at least, he had made a very good point.

"See what happens!" added Yoki enthusiastically. "People try hard to hide their problems from all those around them and to appear happy and content the whole time. They are trying to protect themselves. But if they would only be more open about things, those around them would be far more sensitive and patient with them!"

"Very true!" inserted Nachum, who usually does not express his opinion in public. That, by the way, is one of the reasons why I appreciate him so much. "If we knew that Chaim had an autistic brother, there is no question that we would be more thoughtful towards him and try to support him..."

"I do not think we can just make do with nice talk," Meni pronounced in his funny accent, "We need to show that it really concerns us – we have to do something!"

"Right," Itzik agreed, "Perhaps we could offer to watch… what did you say is his name?" Itzik looked for me in the crowd.

"Mordechai, Motty, or Motek," I replied, giving them all the options.

"Yes," continued Itzik, "we could look after Motek in their home. We could take him every now and again to the playground or something like that."

At the end of the discussion, I was given the duty of informing Chaim that we all were aware of his brother's condition and that we are willing to give a hand to the best of our abilities.

As soon as school was over, I headed straight for Chaim's house. He seemed a bit surprised at my appearance, but because he had not returned to class that day, I did not have the opportunity to arrange my visit with him beforehand.

He invited me in and signaled that I should speak quietly. "He finally fell asleep," he whispered with a half smile. It was clear that he was referring to Motek.

"What do you mean by 'finally?'" I whispered back.

"Don't ask!" said Chaim with a bitter smile. "He put on a real show for us today. He began to go wild, and when my mother tried to calm him, he ran into his room and slammed the door. Somehow, the lock of the door slipped out of place and the door was locked firmly shut. When that happens, the door can only be opened from inside the room. But it would be impossible to expect Motek to open it by himself. You can only imagine what sort of panic my mother went into.

"She called my father to come home from work and they both stood outside the door, not knowing what to do. They called Motek repeatedly. But he, as usual, was lost in his silence and did not utter a sound. They suddenly remembered that there was a small opening located next to the window. It used to hold an air conditioning unit, but was now blocked with thin plywood. That's why they called me home from school – so that I could wriggle through the opening into the room."

Chaim looked at me teary-eyed. "Why am I driving you crazy with these silly stories?" he excused himself. "The main thing is that it's all over."

I told Chaim about our class discussion that day while he was away. I repeated the various points that the boys expressed and informed him of our group decision.

Chaim stared at me as if he could not believe what he was hearing. Within seconds his eyes filled with tears.

"In my wildest dreams, I could not have imagined that the boys in our class would have such a thoughtful reaction!" he exclaimed in a choked voice.

Well, I will not tire you with all the details, but everything worked out unbelievably well. We set up a rotation between all the boys in the class to help look after Motek during the evening hours, as well as on Fridays and *Shabbos*. Even Meni who, as described earlier, does not live in our neighborhood, insisted on being included in the rotation despite having to arrive back home extremely late on those days.

What should I say? Even now, as I am telling you this story, I am deeply moved.

I feel that Chaim and Motek managed to bring out the best in us – and I mean everyone in our grade – as human beings and as Jews.

Reb Chaim

It is amazing to see how people can change so drastically. Chaim is an excellent example. You would not believe how much he developed over the past few weeks. It is as if a new soul entered his body. He now listens attentively in class and actively participates in the discussions. The results have been remarkable!

Thinking back, it is all due to the efforts of our "Tester," Rabbi Shimon. It seems that he succeeded in finding the key that unlocked Chaim's heart and caused him to believe that with a strong will, he too can achieve brilliantly in his studies. Rabbi Shimon's willingness to reveal his amazing life story to us clearly was not in vain. My esteem for Rabbi Shimon has recently grown even stronger.

Last Thursday, the Tester decided to challenge us in a unique way. He asked us to solve a difficulty that arose from the commentary of *Rashi* to the *Gemara* that we were studying.

"This is an extremely difficult question. It was originally posed by Reb Chaim (meaning Rabbi Chaim Solveitchik, or 'Reb Chaim Brisker' for short). I do not expect you to find an immediate solution or even to solve the problem on your own. I strongly encourage you to involve your father or older brother, if you have an older brother, to help you search for an answer."

Nachum asked the Tester to repeat the difficulty, which he did in his usual joyful and enthusiastic way. I now understood the problem better than before. According to Reb Chaim, *Rashi's* commentary completely contradicted the *Gemara*'s statement just two pages earlier.

A wave of excitement washed over me. I really enjoy receiving a serious challenge, and even better – succeeding in solving one.

I absolutely must find an answer for this question, I decided with determination.

Apart from the great challenge, I also wanted to impress the Tester, our teacher, and all of my friends in the grade. I allow myself to presume that similar thoughts were going through my friends' heads at that time.

After Nachum, Chaim asked the Tester to clarify part of his question.

"Please explain once more exactly what you don't understand about Reb Chaim's question," responded the Tester.

At this point, Chaim seemed slightly embarrassed. Instead of explaining Reb Chaim's difficulty with *Rashi*, our teacher wanted to clarify his – Chaim's – own question!

After Chaim overcame his embarrassment and repeated his problem with the original question, a broad smile spread across the face of Rabbi Shimon.

"My dear students," he exclaimed, "I am simply amazed. I am very amazed that we have just merited to hear the very answer that Reb Chaim Brisker gives to this riddle. Yes, our Chaim here – perhaps from now on we should call him 'Reb Chaim' as well – provided the correct answer without even putting great thought into it!"

It soon became clear that the reason why Chaim could not understand the question of Reb Chaim Brisker was because he understood *Rashi* differently to begin with. According to Chaim's interpretation, there could be no problem at all. And that was exactly what Reb Chaim Brisker suggested as his solution to the difficulty.

The Tester rose from his seat and approached Chaim with his hand stretched out in a warm sign of esteem. Chaim did not know where to turn. He flushed red to the roots of his hair and a small ripple of a smile danced across his tightly closed lips. The truth is that Chaim managed to surprise all of us. Personally, I felt a little strange. On the one hand, I was delighted for Chaim. At the same time, I envied him a bit...

Rabbi Shimon then explained the solution to the class once more. He then expanded on the approach taken by Reb Chaim Brisker. From what he said, I understood that one of the main elements of Reb Chaim's approach is to clarify the root of each law and to understand its inner logic.

"For whoever is interested in a better understanding of Reb Chaim Brisker's approach to study," added the Tester, "which,

by the way, is the approach adopted by most of the *yeshivos* in the world, I would suggest buying the book *Ishim VeShitos* by *HaRav* Zevin and carefully examining the chapter that deals with this."

Rabbi Shimon added a story by way of illustration:

Once, Reb Chaim Brisker sat at a convention of Torah scholars, listening to their Torah thoughts and explaining his own. At one point, someone pointed out that a statement made by the commentary of *Tosefos* in a particular *Gemara* undermines what Reb Chaim had just explained. Without hesitation, Reb Chaim replied that there was no such statement in *Tosefos*. Someone then fetched the *Gemara* under dispute and determined that Reb Chaim was correct.

Reb Chaim then turned to those present and declared, "Do you think I am fluent in the entire commentary of *Tosefos* to know what is or is not written in each *Gemara*? Not at all! Rather, I simply understood that a statement such as the one attributed to *Tosefos* just a minute ago could not possibly be correct. The *Tosefos* would not have written such a thing, because the statement contradicts the essential logic of the matter..."

The amazing change in Chaim really got me thinking. I came to the sudden realization that within each of us there are hidden potentials that are generally not used. I wondered whether I had potentials that were waiting to be revealed. You see, I spend much of my time looking at those around me with my "three-dimensional glasses," trying to figure out what is hidden inside. I now tried to turn my gaze inward – into myself. Perhaps I am also capable of achieving much more?

After school, I walked home with my friend Nachum – whom I told you a little about earlier. I am certain that if you knew him, you would also be blown away by his personality. Nachum has a wide, high forehead and grey eyes with a very deep look. Nachum does not only appear to be wise – he *is,* in fact, extremely intelligent. I shared my thoughts with him and he said that he could relate to them. As we walked and spoke about unused potential, an idea suddenly popped into my mind.

"Tell me," I suggested, "why don't we meet up each evening and learn another *Gemara* – not the same one that we already learn in class?"

Nachum surprised me with his quick response.

"It's a deal," he announced, in his usual calm and quiet tone.

We agreed to begin that very evening, Thursday night.

• • •

At the hour that Nachum and I had agreed, I arrived at the *shul.* Nachum was already waiting for me there. He sat by a large table along the left side of the *shul*, with an open *Gemara* in front of him. We had debated which *Gemara* to study earlier, over the phone, and we had eventually settled on *Gemara Brochos*. That way, we reasoned, we would advance our knowledge of the *Halachas* of reciting *brochos*.

The moment I sat down, Nachum began reading the opening words of the first *Mishneh* – "At what time does the obligation of reciting the *Shema* begin at night…?"

Nachum is a very decisive boy – he knows what he wants, focuses on his goal, and wastes no time in getting down to business. He is also capable of joining us in light conversation, but once he decides to study, nothing else exists – no jokes.

We studied for half an hour. My father warned me to go easy at the start. "Don't jump too high at once. A person should only set himself challenges that he is capable of reaching," he explained before I left the house.

We studied an entire page of *Gemara* and it was extremely enjoyable. It is always so much more fun to study a subject that we are not required to study at the moment. We closed our books and chatted quietly for a while. At the same time, I looked around the *shul* and noticed a number of surprising facts.

Firstly, I must point out that until that evening I had no idea what the *shul* looked like at that late hour on an ordinary evening. I now discovered that it literally teemed with life at night.

In the northeastern corner, the *Rav* gave a Torah class in *Shulchan Aruch* to an impressively large audience. Not far away, Reb Dovid ("the wealthy") and Yossel the *Gabbai* sat and studied together. Other seats in the *shul* were taken by men studying alone or with a study partner.

What surprised me more than anything else was the sight of Reb Avraham (the supermarket owner) studying diligently with Ephraim (who works in the iron factory).

"What? Don't you know?" Nachum whispered to me, "ever since they began constructing the school *shul* together, the two of them have become close friends."

I was very touched to hear that. I watched them as they studied. To me, this was the perfect example of our *chachomim's* teaching that "one good deed brings another in its wake."

On our way home, we passed the kiosk of Reb Reuven. It was a small kiosk from which he sold basic food items – bread, milk, oil, and the like. Reb Reuven was an elderly man, lively and good-natured. On *Shabbos*, he would distribute candies in the *shul* to the children who answered *Amen* properly.

Reb Reuven was preparing to close his kiosk for the night. He would close up just before the time for *minchah* each day, only to reopen it later at night, after *maariv*. It was open for one hour each night, in case someone urgently needed some basic supplies after all the other stores were closed.

"Good evening, Reuven!" we called out as we passed him.

"Good evening, my friends!" he responded.

"Where are you returning from at this late hour?" he added with interest.

We told him about our newly created nightly study session.

"Wonderful!" he exclaimed in delight, "you are real *bochrim*!" His two eyes sparkled. "Come inside with me for a minute," he invited.

We entered his kiosk and he handed each of us a bottle of soda.

"This is because I love the Torah and I love those who study the Torah!" he relished, beaming from ear to ear.

"Thank you so much… but it is really unnecessary!" I answered.

"We are not studying to seek rewards," added Nachum.

"If so," replied Reuven in a victorious tone, "then you deserve an even greater reward!" He burst into delighted laughter. "But you should know that it is extremely important to be consistent in your study sessions. If you have agreed to study each evening, then you must be punctual and not allow any excuses to prevent you from attending. The moment you begin with delays and cancellations, there will be no end to them!"

We expressed our agreement.

"Do you know?" he added, "Something very interesting once happened to me, which shows the importance of careful timekeeping in learning and *davening*."

I glanced at my watch. There were just ten minutes left until the time that I promised my parents I would be home.

"It happened between twenty and thirty years ago," Reb Reuven began to recount. "When I was living in Ramat Gan, I owned a store that sold household accessories and gifts. One evening, a customer that I did not recognize entered my store. The man began walking around, examining every single item. He asked where the merchandise came from, he checked all the prices, and every now and again he placed an item on the counter.

"At five to eight, I urged him to hurry. I told him that I close the store at eight o'clock sharp. He acted as if he did not hear me and continued as before. By now, the counter contained a significant amount of items that the man seemed interested in purchasing.

"A minute before closing time, I again informed the man that if he wanted to buy something he would have to hurry, because in another minute I would close the store.

"'But you see that I have not yet finished,' he complained.

"'So come back tomorrow and complete your purchase,' I gently advised.

"He fixed me with an astonished stare and asked, 'Tell me, how often do you have a customer who wants to buy such a quantity of items, that you are prepared to loose a large sale like that?'

"I looked at him and carefully chose my words. The man did not wear a *yarmulka* and I had no way to determine what he did or did not know about Torah and *mitzvos*.

"'Listen, my anonymous friend,' I began jokingly with a sympathetic smile, 'For years now, night after night, I have made certain to attend the evening prayers in the local synagogue over there,' and I pointed across the road towards the *shul* building, 'and after the prayers I join the communal Torah class. The evening prayers begins in exactly five minutes from now and I do not intend to miss it, nor the class after it, for however many shekels you want to pay me! Where does one's livelihood come from if not from G-d...?'

"It was clear that the man was struggling to understand what I had said. An idea suddenly popped into my head. I removed the key to the store from my pocket and placed it on the counter.

"'Here you go!' I declared, 'if it is so urgent for you to make the purchase today, then stay here and continue choosing what you want. Prepare a list of items and come back tomorrow to pay.

Just don't forget to lock the store behind you and to return the key to me when you are done.'

"With that, I gestured towards the exact location of the *shul*. I then hurried to lock the cash register and I ran across the road to the *shul*."

Reb Reuven's story was absolutely fascinating, but its conclusion was more surprising still...

"Towards the end of the *davening*, the customer appeared at the *shul*. He stood there with the key in his hand. I approached him and he handed me the key, but then he remained standing still. I thought that he might be interested in entering the *shul*. I handed him a *yarmulka* and invited him to join me.

"'What did you say that they do here after prayers – study Torah?' he asked. I explained exactly what we study and he decided to remain there for the session."

Reb Reuven suddenly looked at the sealed bottles in our hands.

"Well, my friends," he demanded, "Say a *bracha*!"

We opened the bottles, recited *shehakol* – to which Reb Reuven responded with a loud, enthusiastic *Amen!* – and took a drink.

"You will not believe what the man told me after the session," Reb Reuven returned to his story, "And you will be even more interested to hear what else I have to share with you…!"

• • •

"What is it?" we both exclaimed.

"When the Torah session ended, the man revealed that he had never intended on buying anything from my store to begin with. He was in fact, an undercover detective of the Israel Tax Authority. He was sent to test the store's operations first-hand, and to determine whether each item purchased was in fact recorded as required by law.

"He told me that his main mission was to suggest that he pay me in cash for his large 'purchase' and then to ask me not to record the transaction, in order to save both of us from having to pay the tax. If he would have succeeded in convincing me, I would have found myself in serious trouble and the future of my store would have been highly questionable."

"But why did he ruin his own mission by disclosing his intentions?" I exclaimed in surprise.

"I asked him the same question," replied Reb Reuven with a broad smile beneath his thick, white moustache. "He explained that once he saw that I considered principles more important than making money, so that for the sake of *davening* and Torah class I was ready to risk losing a large profit, he realized that I was not the type of person who was interested in any scams."

"What a wonderful story!" I concluded.

"But what is the other interesting thing that you were going to tell us?" asked Nachum.

Reb Reuven examined him with his kind eyes and kept silent for a few moments, to increase our level of suspense.

"The truly astonishing thing is that you know this man very well!" he announced at last.

"Whom do we know?" we inquired in confusion.

"The undercover detective from the Tax Authority," he replied.

"What do you mean…? We know him…? Who is he?"

"The 'tall Klein' from the wool factory. Do you know him?"

"Of course we know him!" we cried at once.

"Very good," responded Reb Reuven, "Well, he is the man!"

"Hold on a minute," I tried to understand, "Are you telling us that Dovid Klein, the tall one, the father of Reb Leizer the teacher – the Klein who is also your in-law – is the same man that you were telling us about in your story?!"

"Exactly!" chuckled Reb Reuven. "I see that you study plenty of *Talmud*. Your mental grasp is sharp and quick!"

Reb Reuven fell silent once again. He looked at us, deriving pleasure from the amazement written all over our faces.

"Okay, let me explain," he continued, running a damp cloth over the empty counter. "The visit to the *shul* on that evening lit a spark in the heart of the undercover detective, Dovid Klein. After all, a spark of faith exists within the heart of every Jew. From time to time, he returned to visit the *shul*. I became good friends with Dovid and I accompanied him and his wife through every step on the journey back to their roots. Within a relatively short time, the two of them began conducting their home in strict accordance with *Halachah*.

"Dovid and his wife were a young couple, and just at that time, they gave birth to their oldest child, a very charming boy. I merited to participate in his *bris milah* and was even honored to be the *sandek* who holds the child during the *bris*.

"Despite the age gap between the Klein family and ours, the friendship between the two families blossomed. Two years after we became acquainted, our youngest daughter was born.

"We moved from Ramat Gan to this community, which had only recently been established. Dovid and his family followed us here. Dovid, "the tall Klein" as he is nicknamed here – found a home that he really liked, and moved in. He quickly determined that the neighborhood was perfectly conditioned to open a wool factory.

"Years later, when the Kleins' oldest son and our youngest daughter had reached marriageable age, we suggested them for each other. They got married, and we closed a circle that began many years before – although not many people know the history of how our friendship began..."

"What a story!" cried Nachum excitedly.

"Sometimes, reality is so very astonishing, that it beats all imagination," I added.

"Very true," responded Reb Reuven, "But we should always remember that the surprise belongs only to us – not to Hashem. After all, Hashem knows and decides everything in advance. Perhaps that makes it even more fascinating!"

"What are you referring to?" I asked, struggling to understand what he was getting at.

"Let us picture that ordinary evening when an unfamiliar face appeared in my store in Ramat Gan and began removing items from the shelves in order to test my honesty. At that time, it had already been decreed in Heaven that in a certain amount of years, the future son of the 'customer' – who walked in without a *yarmulka* on his head – and the future daughter of the storeowner – who was hurrying to the *shul* – would marry and create a faithful Jewish home together.

"Well, don't you find that absolutely fascinating…?" he concluded.

"You bet!" I confirmed in sheer amazement.

"However, the main message that we must take from this entire story," said Reb Reuven with a smile, waving his finger in the air, "and that is the truly important thing – is that you two boys diligently maintain your new learning session together each evening…!"

Secrets in the Books

The *Yom Tov* of *Pesach* is approaching and my heart is singing with joy. You have no idea how much I love this *Yom Tov* and the entire season. As soon as I hear the term "spring," I immediately envision trees whose branches have been bare for too long, suddenly clothing themselves anew with fresh leaves and decorating themselves with blossoms in a blaze of color.

I deeply enjoy the green plants that appear like small stalks of barley. They sprout wildly and flood the grassy areas at this time of the year.

By the way, I once asked Chaim for the name of those plants and he immediately replied, "Wall Barley." A few years ago, I gathered a handful of wall barley seeds and tried to grind them between two stones to produce flour. My efforts were met with total failure...

What I enjoy most of all – and if you find this amusing, then by all means, go ahead and laugh – is dusting off the *seforim*. At home, this job is reserved for me, because everyone knows how much I enjoy doing it. My father has a large number of *seforim,* and dusting them is an enormous task. I have been doing it for three years now, and with each passing year, the work becomes more systematic. I created a fixed method of cleaning, starting with a particular shelf, removing a specific amount of books at a time, choosing an appropriate corner to dust in, carefully wiping the books, and then returning the books to the shelves in the precise order in which I had originally found them.

Despite my systematic method of dusting, the project takes me longer each year. That is because I do not only dust them – I also inspect their contents. I especially enjoy reading the title pages and prefaces. The information they provide teaches me a lot about the great Torah scholars who authored those *seforim*. I discover their full names, the eras in which they lived, the names of ancient printing houses, and other interesting information.

Sometimes, I can even discover a real secret concealed between the pages. In fact, that is precisely what happened last year.

• • •

As I said, this occurred during the days before *Pesach* of last year. I dusted off my father's *seforim,* and every now and again – whenever my curiosity was aroused – I examined the content of a random book.

I remember being attracted to the contents of a book entitled *Shem HaGedolim*, which I browsed for quite a while. The book was written by the *Chida* – Rabbi Chaim Yosef Dovid Azulai. It was a kind of encyclopedia that reviewed the lives of more than one thousand and three hundred saintly Jewish personalities spanning many generations.

Did you know, for instance, that when someone mentions the *Ravad*, he should specify which *Ravad* he refers to – because there are in fact, three Torah sages with this abbreviated name? The famous *Ravad* who penned a commentary to the *Rambam*'s *Mishneh Torah* is also known as "the third *Ravad*." This is just one example of the type of knowledge that I gained from thumbing through *Shem HaGedolim*.

Some of the books I discovered had accompanied my father since his childhood. They left a great impression on me, because they afforded me a peek into the childhood life of my father.

I discovered *seforim* that he had received as gifts for his birthdays or as prizes for good behavior from his parents – *Sabba* Zalman, of blessed memory, and *Savta* Devorah, may she live a long life.

An old set of *Mikraos Gedolos* bore the inscription, "To our beloved Tzviki on your 12th birthday – until 120!" It was signed, "From *Abba* and *Ima*, who love you forever!" The message in another book read, "To our dear Tzviki, the one and only – may you always continue to give us *nachas*!"

There were *seforim* that he received for outstanding performance in his studies in *cheder* or *yeshivas erev*. On one of the first pages of a set of *Shitah Mekubetzes*, I discovered the following lines: "*Menachem-Av* 5730. To our precious and esteemed student Tzvi Hirsh, for outstanding diligence in your studies at *yeshivas erev* during the past year. Continue ever stronger! – The Administration."

Well, is it not charming to discover that your father was a good boy and an excellent student?

There were also many *seforim* that he received for his *bar mitzvah*, and many others that he picked up from a variety of *genizos*, where old and used *seforim* are discarded. Father acquired a large quantity of *seforim* as an inheritance from his father, *Sabba* Zalman. I merited meeting *Sabba* Zalman, although I cannot recall his actual appearance. To our great sorrow, he passed away when I was just four and a half years old.

• • •

I then picked up a *sefer* entitled *Toldos Yaakov Yosef*, which was authored by Rabbi Yaakov Yosef Katz of Polnoye, one of the original students of the Baal Shem Tov. If I am not mistaken, this *sefer* was one of the first books of *Chassidus* to be published. The *sefer* was old and its pages had turned yellow. In various places, it showed signs of having been eaten by moths. It had been wrapped in nylon and placed on the highest shelf, on top of all the other *seforim*.

I searched for the inscription, which I found written in a beautiful, rounded script. It read: "To my dear husband Zalman, on the second anniversary of our marriage and the birth of our firstborn daughter, Feige. Please accept this gift that I offer you with full intent and feeling."

In my imagination, I pictured *Savta* Devorah as a very young woman purchasing this *sefer* and presenting it as a gift to her husband, *Sabba* Zalman. It seems that back then it was the women who bought gifts for their husbands, I noted with a smile.

There was something about the inscription that I failed to understand. It mentioned that the oldest daughter of *Sabba* and *Savta* was named Feige. Now, my father (the youngest of his siblings) has one brother and three sisters – none of whom are named Feige.

The mystery only deepened when I noticed – and I cannot imagine why I failed to notice this before – that the inscription was signed by someone with the name Chavah. I rubbed my eyes and looked again. The inscription was still there, with a Feige and a Chavah. There could be no mistaking the names because the inscription was written in a beautifully clear handwriting. "Chavah," it read – absolutely not "Devorah."

Perhaps I was mistaken to assume that "my dear husband Zalman" referred to my grandfather. Perhaps it meant a different Zalman? This book could have been just one of the many that my father collected from a *genizah*.

However, that possibility seemed quite unlikely to me. If the old, shabby book in my hand was not acquired by inheritance from my grandfather, and if it did not carry great sentimental value to my own father, then it is reasonable to assume that he would not have insisted on keeping it in the house. I gently returned the book to its transparent packaging, and resolved to clarify the issue with my father.

"That book up there, the one in a nylon wrap," I questioned my father at the first opportunity while pointing to the highest shelf, "Did it belong to *Sabba* Zalman?"

"Which book – the *Toldos*?" he asked.

"Yes, *Toldos Yaakov Yosef*," I replied.

"Uh-huh," he intoned. I believe that I sensed a sort of tension in his voice.

"So who is Chavah?" I asked, adding in the same breath, "And who is Feige?"

My question seemed to confuse him.

"What do you mean 'who?' Why are you asking anyway?" he asked, clearly trying to buy time to sort out his thoughts.

"Because the woman who presented the book to her husband, *Sabba* Zalman, signed her name as Chavah instead of her actual name, Devorah," I responded. "Apart from that, she also mentioned the birth of their firstborn daughter Feige, and I do not know of any aunt with that name."

"Okay… You see…" Father tried to avoid answering, "This story… Umm… This story is a bit… Basically, let's push off discussing this until a more appropriate, calmer time. Right now, I have a number of urgent matters to take care of."

His reply sounded like an awkward way of avoiding the issue. It only increased my curiosity. I sensed that I had stumbled upon a serious discovery. I had no choice but to wait for a more opportune time...

My opportunity was not long in coming. It was on one of the nights of *Chol HaMoed Pesach*. Towards evening, the entire family returned from a pleasant trip to the Ktalav Valley in the Judean Hills. I accompanied my father to *maariv*. On the way home from *shul*, I asked him delicately whether the "more appropriate time" had come yet, and whether it would not bother him to explain the riddle of the inscription in the old copy of the *Toldos* to me.

"You don't give up, do you?" my father blurted out with a smile. He patted me on the shoulder.

Just a few feet away from our house, there is a bench that is positioned under the shade of a giant sycamore tree. On the tree, a small plaque from the Nature Reserves Authority announces, "Protected Tree."

"Shall we sit here?" suggested Father. We sat down on the bench.

"Do you see this sycamore tree?" my father asked suddenly. "There were once sycamores growing all over this area. Then people began using them for carpentry and the sycamores were almost eradicated from our land. This lucky tree, however, has a long history and is rooted extremely deeply in the ground."

The unexpected lesson in botany took me by surprise.

My father continued, "We humans also have a history and roots that are important to recognize. Well, I assume that you know very little about *Sabba* Zalman..."

"That's right," I replied, as the purpose of his "lesson" sunk in. "All I know about him is that he was born in a town next to Warsaw, the capital city of Poland. He later came to Israel and raised a family together with *Savta* Devorah."

"Okay," my father chuckled, "It seems that even the little information you do have about him is not entirely accurate. Come, let's sort this all out. I will tell you a bit about the life of *Sabba* and from what you hear you will also receive the answers to your questions."

He then began to tell a tale...

"*Sabba* Zalman was born in Otwock, a town not far from the city of Warsaw. When the Second World War broke out, he was fifteen years old. Hitler, the leader of the German Nazis (may his name be eradicated), annexed the neighboring country of Austria and conquered Czechoslovakia and parts of Lithuania. It was clear that Poland was next in line to be conquered by Germany – that actually happened just a little later.

"A few months before that, Zalman's parents (my grandparents) decided to arrange for their son to escape from Europe. Zalman's father had a brother living in America. His name was Yosef, but ever since arriving in America he adopted the nickname Jo. In one of his letters to Otwock, Uncle Jo suggested that Zalman be sent to live with him until the end of the war. 'There are *yeshivos* in America as well,' wrote Jo in his letter, 'and I take upon myself to find him a suitable *yeshivah* and to care for all his needs.'

"With an extremely heavy heart, my grandparents accepted the offer. They separated from their son with the hope that they would merit to see him immediately after the war. The young teenager set out alone on his journey to America.

"*Sabba* Zalman was welcomed warmly into the family of his uncle, who lived in a city in Mississippi – one of the southern states of America. Shortly after arrival, he began studying in a *yeshivah* in the neighboring state of Tennessee. He would return to the home of his aunt and uncle only once a month, generally traveling by train.

"Uncle Jo owned a large cotton plantation. When his nephew would return from *yeshivah*, Jo would ask him to lend a hand on the plantation. Ever grateful to his aunt and uncle, his benefactors, Zalman was delighted at the chance to pay them back with a favor, and so he always helped them out on the plantation. Over the next few years, he continued to study in the *yeshivah* and work on the cotton plantation.

"Finally, when Germany was beaten by the Allied Forces and the War had ended, the entire world discovered the true extent of the horrifying, unbelievable murder and brutality of the Holocaust. Accurate testimony emerged from Otwock, bringing to Zalman – who had by then matured into a young man – the bitter news: The Nazis had murdered his entire family. He and his aunt and uncle were all that remained of his once large and distinguished extended family.

"Zalman decided to remain in America and build his future there. Two years after the War, he married a young lady named Chavah."

My father paused for a moment to note my response to his last sentence. You could say that I was in complete shock.

"Are you saying that *Savta* Devorah was not *Sabba* Zalman's first wife?" I exclaimed, trying to digest the astonishing information.

"Correct," my father nodded.

"So what happened to her – I mean Chavah?" I asked with a strange sensation.

"We will get to that right now," he replied. "One year after their marriage, they had a daughter whom they named Feige after the mother of *Sabba* Zalman – she had been killed in the Holocaust, as mentioned."

I could not control myself. "Where is Feige?" I blurted out.

"You don't need to press me," my father gently replied, understanding my strong emotion. "I will tell you everything."

"Uncle Jo was not growing any younger as time passed and he required more and more help on his plantation. On the other hand, *Sabba* Zalman was now a husband and a father, and he needed to provide for his family. He began to divide his days between learning Torah in the *shul* – which was nothing more than a shabby hut that served the small community of local Jews – and working in the cotton fields.

"Then one day, something awful happened."

Father's tone changed. He swallowed hard.

"One of Jo's workers, a black man who was deaf in one ear, was driving a giant tractor on the grounds of the plantation. At the same time, Chavah and little Feige were strolling at the back of their house that was located at the edge of the plantation. The worker confused the tractor's controls for a moment and instead of moving forward, he put the tractor into reverse. Chavah and Feige were crushed to death..."

"Oyyy!" I cried out spontaneously, trembling all over.

"It was a terrible, awful tragedy. I cannot even describe it in words," father sighed deeply.

"The tragedy totally shattered *Sabba* Zalman. He told me that he was unable to leave the house for weeks on end. He was completely consumed with unbearable grief. He was not willing to see or hear anyone. He felt that the calamity that befell his family had chased after him even to America and had caught up with him there. In Poland, he lost his father, mother, and the rest

of his family. Now, the new family that he had begun to raise with great difficulty was tragically killed.

"Who succeeded in removing *Sabba* Zalman from his profound state of brokenhearted grief? His aunt and uncle. They advised him to travel to the Holy Land and begin a new life. At first, *Sabba* Zalman was extremely hesitant. He did not know anyone, nor did he have any relatives there. In the end, though, he was convinced. 'A change of location brings a change of fortune,' he told himself. He hoped that in Israel he would finally succeed in starting a new and more fortunate chapter to his life."

"And that is precisely what happened – no?" I mumbled hesitantly.

"Yes, *Boruch Hashem*!" replied Father with a smile. "*Sabba* immigrated to Israel and not long afterwards he married *Savta* Devorah, may she live many good years. He truly felt that his fortune improved immensely by his move to the Holy Land. On the ruins of his tragic past, *Sabba* built a wonderful family that provided him with at least some measure of comfort for the many tragedies that he suffered, and that filled his heart with pride and joy."

Father suddenly rose from the bench. I did the same. A pleasant breeze was blowing, as the two of us began walking towards our house.

"For decades, *Sabba* refused to speak about his tragic life," Father explained, "until one time, he unexpectedly opened up and told everything."

"Wait a minute!" Father exclaimed. I detected a note of passion in his voice. "As I am telling you all this, I have just remembered that the discussion between *Sabba* Zalman and me, also took place during *Pesach*. Isn't it unbelievable how things truly come full circle in this world…?

"It happened one year, right after the *Seder*. Everyone else had already gone to bed. Only *Sabba* and I remained sitting by the table. All of a sudden, without any prior warning, he began telling me the story of his life in Europe and America. 'I don't know why, but I always remember this on the night of the *Seder*,' *Sabba* said, wiping tears from his eyes."

Father and I ascended the small staircase that brought us to the door of our home. A peaceful silence hovered over the neighborhood. Only the crickets disturbed the quiet night. I wanted to say something and searched for the right words.

"This is a literal fulfillment of the *Pesach* obligation, 'and you shall tell it to your son,'" I said at last with a smile. "It seems that the festival of *Pesach* is the time for fathers to tell their sons their stories..."

At that moment, we crossed the threshold of our house.

And that, my dear friends, is the story that I discovered last year while dusting my father's large collection of *seforim*. You can just imagine what an opportunity I would have lost if I would have not come across that *sefer,* or if I would not have opened it and peeked inside.

That is precisely why I told you that there are real secrets concealed between the pages of these *seforim*.

Separated Twins

It is not every day that our neighborhood receives a new resident, and certainly not a new *senior* resident.

The issue is really quite straightforward. Our neighborhood is already filled to capacity and there are hardly any new buildings. For years now, there has been talk of building a new neighborhood to the west of ours, but the plans seemed to have stalled permanently. The main obstacle results from the fact that our neighborhood is surrounded by agricultural land. It is a complicated process to convert an agricultural area into a residential one.

A number of young men – not too many – built additional houses as attachments to their parents' homes, shortly after their marriages. A handful of residents also built small extensions in their yards to rent. Anyway, this is not the main point.

The story that I would like to tell is about Yaakov. As I mentioned, he is an elderly man. I would estimate that he is about seventy-five. Yaakov is a tall, thin man, who wears a *kasket*. He arrived in our neighborhood two months ago and settled in a small room at the back of Rabbi Meir Rosenberg's house. Rabbi Rosenberg is the head of the neighborhood's *Kolel* for seniors.

Nobody knows exactly who he is, where he came from, or why he moved into our neighborhood. The truth is that nobody seems overly interested in finding out. But you know that you can rely on my curious nature not to let such a matter slip past without discovering its details.

I did not unravel the "Yaakov Mystery" in one day. It took a lot of effort and the painstakingly slow work of putting together the pieces of the puzzle until I could see the full picture. Believe me, it was well worth the effort. The story that I uncovered is the kind of tale that fits the saying, "Reality is stranger than fiction."

In order for you to also appreciate the full picture, please allow me to take you back many decades in time. I will begin the story from the very beginning.

• • •

Twin brothers Max and Jack were born in the German city of Furstenberg. They were handsome blond haired boys. Their parents were Jewish and considered themselves part of the local Jewish community, which like many other Jewish communities in Germany, was extremely modern and assimilated.

When the Second World War broke out, Max and Jack were just one year old. Within a short time, the Nazis began rounding up the Jews of Germany and shipping them off to extermination camps. Moments before the parents of Max and Jack were gathered in the main square of their city and then transported to a camp called Sachsenhausen (not far from Berlin), they decided to do something unthinkable. They really had no other choice. The only way to save the lives of their two tiny children was to hand their young boys over for adoption to two gentile neighbors with whom they had been friendly for many years.

Max was adopted by Otto and Bertha Steinbruk, an intellectual couple who were already parents of two boys of their own – aged nine and ten.

Jack was adopted by Angela Krainski who had refused to remarry after the sudden death of her husband. She did not have children of her own and desperately wished to have a child whom she could love and raise. That was her deeper reason for accepting the great risk of sheltering a Jewish child in her house.

The two young toddlers had no way of knowing that before they had reached the age of three they were already orphaned from both their mother and father. Their father died of typhus in a concentration camp. Their mother was killed as she tried to escape from the camp.

Equally heartrending is the fact that the twins grew up living so very close to each other, but neither knew about the other. The Steinbruks and Mrs. Krainski purposely hid that fact from them in order to keep their Jewish identities secret and protect their lives. They even arranged between themselves to dress the boys very differently and to give them dissimilar hairstyles to look less identical.

Twice during the course of the war, SS officials visited Angela's home and questioned her over Jack's identity, because his name did not appear in the official records as her son. Angela insisted that the boy was indeed her son. Somehow, these visits ended peacefully. On the other hand, the Steinbruk family never received such visits. Otto Steinbruk was a popular and distinguished figure in the city and nobody doubted his honesty or his loyalty to the regime.

Towards the end of the war, Max and Jack were six years old. They were sent to study in two different schools. News of the fate of the Jews of Germany, and particularly of Furstenberg, reached the ears of the foster parents of the twin boys. They realized that after the war someone might possibly come looking for the boys to return them to their families.

Bertha would gaze at Max every now and again. She had raised him and watched him grow in her care. Her heart ached. The mother of little Max had been her true friend and she had great respect for his father as an upright, honest and goodhearted man. She was deeply pained for Max and grieved for the terrible fate of his parents.

Angela, on the other hand, was embarrassed to admit that to a certain degree she was pleased to hear the news that Jack's parents would not return to take him from her. Now she would truly have a child to raise as her own. In order to quiet her conscience, Angela convinced herself that Jack would have a much brighter future if she continued to raise him as a gentile German boy.

Certainly, she was appalled at the barbaric murder inflicted on the Jews by Hitler and his soldiers, but what could she do to change the situation? In a world where Jews are killed just because they are Jews, she reasoned, perhaps it would be better for Jack not to know that he is a Jew. She decided to raise him as if he were her own child in every regard.

The war finally ended. By now, Max and Jack were happy and delightful seven year olds. Otto and Bertha Steinbruk were

determined to do everything possible to locate the relatives of Max and hand him over to their care.

"The boy was born Jewish and he should be allowed to grow as a Jew!" Bertha told her husband. Otto agreed completely.

Within a few months, they succeeded in locating an aunt of Max, his father's sister Sarah, and sent Max to live with her. Sarah had been in a concentration camp during the war and had been freed when the war ended. She received her young nephew with open arms. Max was her only relative to survive the Holocaust. All her other family members had been murdered.

At the same time, the Steinbruks decided not to tell Sarah who had adopted the twin brother of Max.

"We do not have the right to remove Jack from Angela, after the great sacrifice that she displayed throughout the war years in raising and protecting him. She really risked her life for him!" they told each other. They reasoned that Angela should be free to make her own choice regarding the future of the little Jewish boy who had been entrusted into her care.

A short while later, Sarah and Max left Germany and set out for the Holy Land, which was then controlled by Britain. Despite the British ban on Jewish immigration at the time, they succeeded in smuggling their way into the country illegally with a group arranged by Jewish activists.

Jack and Max, the separated twin brothers, now began entirely dissimilar lives.

• • •

Unlike her brother and sister-in-law, the parents of Max, Aunt Sarah was very *frum*. With the help of kind individuals, she succeeded in finding a small room to rent for her nephew and herself in the Meah Shearim neighborhood of Yerusholayim where the environment matched her *frum* lifestyle.

From the moment he stepped foot in Meah Shearim, Max was called by his original Jewish name – Meir. He was immediately enrolled in a *cheder*. The transition from his non-Jewish school in the German city of Furstenberg to the *cheder* was not at all easy. Luckily, he discovered that his fluency in German helped him pick up the local language – Yiddish.

Meir also experienced the many hardships of the Jewish settlement in Yerusholayim in those early days. Within a couple of years, Meir looked and acted no different from any other boy in Meah Shearim. He entered *yeshivah* at the age of thirteen and performed well in his learning. After graduating *Yeshivah Ketanah* he entered *Yeshivah Gedolah*. When he came of age, he married and raised a family.

His aunt Sarah also got married, although she did not have any children. A few years after her marriage, her husband died a sudden death. Sarah was not left entirely alone, because her nephew Meir was like a devoted son to her, and his children were considered her own grandchildren in every way.

Forty years or so had passed since Sarah and Meir (Max) arrived in Israel. Sarah had grown elderly and frail. Meir and his wife enthusiastically suggested that she come live with them, but she absolutely refused to hear about it.

"I do not want to be a burden on you," she insisted. "Hashem has helped me through everything until now and He will help me in the future as well!"

Sarah researched and located a home for the elderly in which to spend the remainder of her life. As a result, Meir and his family moved into our neighborhood, which was the closest neighborhood to the facility in which Sarah was living. They wanted to be as near as possible to Sarah. Ever since then – and that was well before I was born – Rabbi Meir Rosenberg has lived in our neighborhood.

The most dramatic development in this story happened just fifteen years ago.

It occurred approximately half a year before Sarah passed away. A letter addressed to Sarah arrived in the mail at her home for the elderly. The letter was handwritten in German. Sarah did not require an interpreter to read it; she was fluent in the language of the country in which she was born and raised.

The letter was written by an elderly woman who lived in the German city of Furstenberg. To my best recollection, this is what was written:

> Dear Mrs. Sarah,
>
> You do not know me because we have never met face to face.
>
> My name is Angela Krainski and I wish to share a secret with you. I know that I will not live forever and I do not want to take this secret with me to the grave.
>
> I was able to reach out to you through the help of my good friend, Mrs. Bertha Steinbruk, the woman who looked after Max throughout the war years. It would probably interest you to know that Bertha is not that young anymore either, although she still functions wonderfully.

Anyway, you are most certainly aware that Max had a twin brother. In fact, he still has a twin brother. His brother Jack was entrusted to my care for the duration of the war by their parents, Mr. Arthur and Mrs. Leiza Rosenberg, whose souls now rest in Paradise.

To my great sorrow, Arthur and Leiza perished in the war and no one came to reclaim Jack from me. I was living all alone and Jack too had no one for him in the world. I had also grown deeply attached to him by the end of the war. For his sake and my own, I decided to continue raising him with great love, as if I had given birth to him myself.

I later discovered through my friend Bertha that she had handed Max into your care. But by then, you were no longer in the area and I also found it difficult to reconsider my original decision.

I am very pained, Mrs. Sarah. I do not know what state of health this letter will find you in (if at all...). Nevertheless, these are the facts. I hope that you will be able to understand me and succeed in forgiving me.

There is one thing that I can promise you. I raised Jack with the utmost warmth and love and he has grown into a healthy and content man.

Until just a few weeks ago, even Jack did not know that he was adopted. I have only recently revealed this secret to him, out of a deep sense of commitment to my conscience. Jack has already turned sixty (as you well know, because that is precisely the age of Max).

When Jack heard the entire story from me, and when I informed him that I was not his actual mother, he dismissed the whole thing with a wave of his hand. He said that did not intend to do anything with the new information that I had given him.

"I am not a young man anymore and I no longer have the strength to begin dealing with a new and unfamiliar reality," he insisted. "Apart from that, if you have been my mother all this time until now, then you will remain that way in the future as well."

Nevertheless, as mentioned, I have decided to inform you of the authentic facts. As I described at the beginning of this letter, it was my friend Bertha who gave me your name and helped me locate your address in Israel.

Be blessed and give my blessings to Max – I still have an excellent recollection of him playing together with Jack in the home of their parents, which was located at 328 Winterfeldstrasse.

Sincerely yours,

Angela

Angela's letter completely disrupted Sarah's tranquility, and took her back fifty years in time. Sarah had never forgotten little Jack, the twin brother of Max. However, since she did not believe that she would ever succeed in locating him, she found it better to push the painful memory of the missing twin out of her mind and not focus on it. She knew that thousands of Jewish children had been lost during the war. Many had ended up in monasteries or in the homes of gentiles who had agreed to hide them. She had assumed that something like that must have happened to Jack.

Now, everything has abruptly opened up again...

The discovery that he had a twin brother who had remained alive all these years – living a completely non-Jewish lifestyle in Germany – hit Rabbi Meir with total shock. Unlike Jack, Rabbi Meir had absolutely no intention of considering the discovery as some kind of dream from which one awakens the next morning and continues with life as if nothing happened.

Rabbi Meir immediately sat down and wrote two letters, one to Angela Krainski and the other to Jack Krainski. His letter to his twin brother was short and restrained. It was designed only as an initial probe. This is what he wrote:

> Undoubtedly, you were as surprised as I was when presented with the new information that your foster-mother revealed. I cannot describe in a single letter all that has happened to me since the time I left Germany and immigrated to Israel. At the same time, I am equally unable to make peace with the fact that in some place in the world – and it really does not matter where – there lives my twin brother, a half of myself, and yet we do not know each other... I think that we should meet somewhere soon. What do you think?

• • •

Jack's reply only arrived in the mailbox of Rabbi Meir two months later.

> I am sorry for the delay in writing and mailing this letter.

> Please do not consider this an insult in the slightest. What happened to cause the delay was that my dear mother – the woman whom I have called "mother" my entire life – died suddenly, just a few days after I received your letter. I was plunged into a state of deep mourning for her, and I focused on trying to come to terms with her passing.

In the continuation of the letter, Jack expressed his willingness to meet his brother, but only in Germany.

> Please understand that I am a professor in the University of Berlin and during the coming months, I am unable to take time off from my work for the sake of travel. I would greatly appreciate your effort in traveling here. You may stay in my house as long as you wish. No one will bother you – there will be only the two of us here.

Rabbi Meir read the letter repeatedly. He tried to discover as many details as possible about his brother from the brief correspondence, reading the lines and between the lines... He racked his brain trying to understand the hint behind the words "No one will bother you – there will be only the two of us here."

Three weeks later, Rabbi Meir landed in the Berlin Tegel Airport. The welcome sign written in German that read "Willkommen Max" was not necessary in the slightest. Jack held the sign at the arrivals terminal to make it easier for the brothers to recognize each other, but even without it, Rabbi Meir would have identified Jack instantly. The distinction in the way they dressed and in their external appearances did not conceal the astonishing similarity between the twins.

Max

With great hesitancy, the brothers stepped toward each other. Jack seemed overly shocked. After the sensational discovery that he was in fact a Jew and that he has a living brother, he now meets this person who appears to be a rabbi – with a beard and a dark hat and suit.

For a long while, they stood opposite each other, each staring at the other. Jack gave a confused smile, but Rabbi Meir was the first to break the ice.

"So," he began, "then *you* are my twin brother!"

Jack's car awaited them at the terminal parking. It was an expensive and new black vehicle. Just an hour and a half after Rabbi Meir had landed in Berlin, the two brothers sat on the sofa in Jack's living room.

"Would you care for a cup of coffee?" Jack offered his brother.

"No, thank you," answered Rabbi Meir with a chuckle, "I have a special diet." He removed from his hand luggage a packet of salted peanuts that he had received during the flight.

The following hours flew past without them realizing. Rabbi Meir opened his suitcase and removed a photo album that he had brought from Israel. He handed it to Jack. The pictures were of Rabbi Meir's childhood and the subsequent stages of his life – his time spent learning in *yeshivah*, his wedding, and his children.

"Here is our eldest daughter Aliza. She is soon to be married," he added as if sharing a secret.

Jack's brow creased. "Aliza… Aliza…" he muttered, trying to recall something. "From where do I know that name?"

"We named her after our late mother, Leiza," Rabbi Meir hurried to explain.

"How right you are!" cried Jack, "My 'mother' indeed mentioned this name to me. Leiza Rosenberg… Arthur and Leiza Rosenberg..."

Jack gazed at his brother and even smiled from time to time, but he seemed to be deeply troubled.

"You know what, Max?" he said suddenly, "I am not sure that if it were up to me, I would have been willing to discover all of this..."

He fell silent for a moment and then continued slowly, emphasizing each word.

"To a great extent I am even angry at my 'mother.' For sixty years, I have lived a certain lifestyle and felt the same as everyone else around me. All of a sudden, like an unpredicted hurricane, this story turns up and threatens to wash away my life and completely drown it..."

Jack stared into the distance out of the living room window and questioned, "Why do I need all this? Why could she not have simply died quietly and left me to lead my life as I have until now?"

Jack sounded bitter and frustrated.

Rabbi Meir looked sympathetically at his twin. "I can absolutely understand you, Jack," he said, "But how does the saying go? 'If fate has decided to chase after you, be certain that it will reach you…'"

"Yes, yes," smiled Jack, "a wise saying."

Jack stood up and withdrew a picture album from a nearby closet. He placed it on the table, opened it and turned it to face his brother.

Young Jack looked like an exact copy of young Max. Jack going to school. Jack sailing on the river Spree in Berlin with his "mother." Jack at his graduation from elementary school. Jack in high school. Jack in university. Jack as a lecturer in university.

Rabbi Meir withheld himself the entire time. One question disturbed him greatly and it grew more powerful with every turn of the page in Jack's album. At a certain point, he could restrain himself no longer.

"Tell me, Jack," he questioned, "when you wrote to me in your letter that I could stay in your house as long as I wish and that 'there will be only the two of us here' – what exactly did you mean?"

Jack gave him a look that betrayed great sadness.

"If you mean to ask whether I was ever married and had children, then the answer is – no. I was far too busy with my career. I did not have time to raise a family. Years later, I regretted it, but by then it was just too late."

Rabbi Meir felt torn between two emotions. On the one hand, he identified with the feelings of pain that his brother was experiencing. At the same time, if his brother had gotten married, then he would have most probably married a non-Jew.

Heaven protected him, Rabbi Meir thought to himself.

"When I look at the album of photographs that you have brought with you," continued Jack, "it is impossible for me not to envy you. You raised a wonderful family while I am left all alone in the world. Alone and lonely." His voice had begun to break.

"Not any more!" Rabbi Meir attempted to encourage him and perhaps find a way into his brother's heart. "You are no longer alone. You have a brother, an aunt, nieces and nephews, and..."

"Stop!" Jack cut him off with a gruff tone of voice. "A person cannot discover that he has family so suddenly, at the age of sixty. It is unnatural and untruthful. A family is not simply a matter of blood relatives and a family tree. A family is an entire system of relationships and feelings."

"Nevertheless," Rabbi Meir persisted, "it is impossible to hide from the fact that we were both born from the same mother and father and that we grew up together until the age of two – until wicked, cruel forces took our parents from us and separated us. Do you want to hand victory to the forces of evil…?"

Jack appeared to be seriously contemplating his brother's words.

"Wait a moment," he suddenly announced in a flash of memory. "I have to show you something..."

Jack disappeared into a nearby room and returned a moment later. In his hand, he held a worn and dusty envelope.

"You will never guess what I have in here," he told his twin secretively.

"What is it?" asked Rabbi Meir in surprise.

"You will see straight away," replied Jack with a small smile on his lips. He sat next to Rabbi Meir and delicately removed the brown wrapping paper from a small scrap of cardboard, which turned out to be an old photograph.

Jack gently blew the dust off the picture. "Please," he said, handing his brother the photograph. It took Rabbi Meir a second, perhaps less, to understand who was in the picture.

"Where… where did you get this picture from?" he stuttered with great emotion.

"From my mother – I mean, my foster-mother," Jack corrected himself. "She told me that Leiza Rosenberg gave her the photograph on the day that she entrusted me to her care."

Rabbi Meir's eyes filled with tears. He gazed at the picture, stunned. Unlike his twin, he knew the names of his true parents his entire life. His aunt Sarah had told him plenty about them. From his earliest childhood, he had attempted to picture in his mind the image of his parents, to dream about them, to feel a sense of connection with them. The unfortunate fact was that he did not remember what they looked like, nor did he have any pictures of them. This prevented him from properly imagining them. Now, completely unexpectedly and at the age of sixty, he finally merited to "see" and "recognize" them.

His father Arthur (Asher) Rosenberg stared at him from the photograph. He appeared young, confident and proud. He wore a tailored suit and a small black hat tilted slightly to one side.

At his father's side, stood his mother Leiza (Aliza). She was slightly taller than his father. Her eyes had a peaceful and goodhearted look, and her mouth wore a smile.

His parents were not the only ones in the touching photograph. At the front of the picture, were golden-haired twin boys. They appeared to be between one and two years old. They wore sailor suits and sat on high-backed chairs.

"That's me," Rabbi Meir told Jack in a choked voice, pointing to one of the twins. "And that's you," he immediately added as he moved his finger towards the face of the other cute child in the picture.

"That's what I thought as well," Jack confirmed. "And look – even then you looked more Jewish than me…" he added, perhaps jokingly, perhaps sarcastically.

Rabbi Meir was silent, lost in his thought. He suddenly drew the picture close to his lips and gave it a most heartfelt kiss. His emotions affected Jack, even for just a moment, and Jack placed his arm around Rabbi Meir's shoulders, his eyes growing somewhat hazy.

Rabbi Meir snapped out of his thoughts. "One moment… In your foster-mother's letter to our aunt Sarah, she mentions a woman who looked after me during the war."

"What are you getting at?" Jack tried to understand.

"Well, she is still alive, isn't she?" asked Rabbi Meir.

"Certainly," replied Jack. "Mrs. Steinbruk has almost reached the age of ninety, but she is alive and active and has an extremely clear head."

"If so, then she may have more information or documents regarding us and our parents!" cried Rabbi Meir excitedly.

"That's possible," answered Jack, completely lacking the enthusiasm of his twin. Jack was hesitant and not at all pleased at having discovered his true family and having to face the shock of the new reality.

After a thoughtful pause, Jack continued, "I will give you her telephone number and address. I have known her all of these years, long before I discovered that she and my foster-mother shared a secret between them. She lives two streets from here and I would assume that she will even be quite pleased to meet you."

Rabbi Meir was pained at the cold indifference of his brother, but tried his best to disguise his disappointment. That very evening, Jack set up a meeting with Mrs. Steinbruk to take place the following morning.

Jack was correct. Bertha was extremely delighted to meet Rabbi Meir.

"Oh, Max – it would be hilarious if I were to say, 'Look how much you have grown!' or 'See how much you have changed!' But one thing I can tell you: You are a carbon copy of your mother..." Bertha wiped a handkerchief over her moist eyes.

Rabbi Meir spent the following hours in the house of the woman who had raised him for five years of his life. He listened to stories about him and his parents and he made multiple use of the box of tissues sitting on the table before him. Bertha gave him a vast amount of information, although she did not have any pictures or documents that related to him or his family.

"You must understand," she explained, "that so many years have passed since those times. I never imagined that I would ever see you again. Even if I did once have something, I doubt that I would have kept it."

Rabbi Meir stayed in his twin's house for five days. They had long fascinating talks that quite often turned into heated debates. In the end, Rabbi Meir failed to convince his twin to recognize his Jewishness and to return to his roots. When they departed from each other at the airport, Rabbi Meir had very mixed feelings.

More than fourteen years passed since their reunion. Throughout that time, the twins were careful to maintain steady contact via telephone and mail.

One day, just over half a year ago, the phone in Rabbi Meir's house rang. Jack was calling from Germany. It was not just another one of their many polite conversations. This time, Jack sounded different. He was in a particularly gloomy mood. He explained that he sensed old age breathing down his neck and his sense of loneliness was stronger than ever before. At the end of the unusual conversation, Jack dropped the bombshell. He said that for a while now he had been weighing his options from every side and angle. He had reached the conclusion that he was ready to introduce a dramatic change to his life.

That conversation triggered a whole series of talks. After everything had been arranged, Jack arrived in Israel.

This, then, was the identity of the elderly newcomer to our neighborhood. It was none other than Jack – or more properly, Yaakov. Yes, Yaakov the professor who had been raised and lived his entire life as a German gentile was in fact the brother of Rabbi

Meir, the head of the *Kolel* in which our neighborhood's elderly residents gathered to study Torah.

As I told you right at the beginning, most of the residents here are not aware of all that I have just told you. As far as they are concerned, the entire "Yaakov Mystery" is only a mystery to my powerful imagination... After all, what could be so interesting about an elderly man who lives in a small room at the back of Rabbi Meir Rosenberg's house…?

A High Standard

Here we go – the *bar mitzvah* season has begun!

After a lengthy period in which the majority of our discussions during recess has focused on *tefillin*, the various *sofrim* who write and sell them, those who fashion the leather *batim* out of cow hide, and when and where each of our *bar mitzvos* will likely be held – we finally reached the very first *bar mitzvah* in the grade.

That honor fell to Elimelech – "the tall." He is not only taller than the rest of us, but he is also the oldest. Mind you, there is only one day between Elimelech's birthday and the birthday of Dudi, a good, quiet and likeable boy. That one day is extraordinarily critical. Just how critical could it be? That will soon be seen...

We have been hearing about the promised magic and glory of Elimelech's *bar mitzvah* for months now; he has not stopped talking about it. Elimelech is not a bad boy – he is good and decent in his own unique way. It is just that he belongs squarely in the category of people who whatever they do must always be the absolute "best."

No doubt, you know a few such people. When they buy clothing, a game or whatever, they must tell everyone that they bought the best brand possible. When their mother or father does something, it is always the very smartest and most appropriate thing to do. Even when they do *not* do anything, their inaction is always based on the most brilliant reasoning available.

And so, the *sofer* who wrote the *parshiyos* that were placed inside Elimelech's *tefillin* had to be the best *sofer* in Israel – "and perhaps in the entire world." We are talking about a veteran *sofer* from Meah Shearim; if a father desires to purchase *parshiyos* from this venerable *sofer* for his son, he must place his order "at least ten years before the child's *bar mitzvah*."

The *batim* for Elimelech's *tefillin* were the most *mehudar batim* available. And their cost? "Sky-high!" Even the holders that for most people are made of plastic, were in this case wooden with a pure silver coating. What about his *tefillin* bag? Don't ask. Those bags were fashioned from "expensive Italian velvet, embroidered with red and gold lettering."

It would be untrue to say that I do not sometimes envy Elimelech. My mother once told me that "it is natural to envy" and one must only be careful "not to mix in jealousy or resentment." For that reason, I do not really have a problem with Elimelech's boasting and showing off. Everyone lives according to their abilities and it would seem that Elimelech's father (who owns the neighborhood's factory that produces storage boxes) is able to live well above the average.

The problem with Elimelech's attitude is that it sets a high standard for the rest of the class. The fact that his *bar mitzvah* is the first in our grade magnifies the problem ten times over. Now each *bar mitzvah* in the class will be compared to his.

Well, from my description of Elimelech's *tefillin*, you can imagine what his actual *bar mitzvah* celebration looked like.

There are two locations in our community in which people hold a *bris milah*, *sheva brochos* or *bar mitzvah*. The first is the women's section of our *shul* and the second is our school assembly hall. The school hall is larger and the choice of location usually depends on the amount of guests.

Elimelech, needless to say, informed us that he has a "gigantic family" that is difficult to squeeze into either of these locations. Aside from this, Elimelech's mother apparently complained that "although it is unpleasant to say, the fact is that neither of these two places are fit to host a respectful event." They were left with no choice but to have the celebration at a location outside of the neighborhood.

So, the first *bar mitzvah* in our grade was held in Luxury Hall (what an appropriate name…), located in the city nearest to our neighborhood.

What can I tell you? It was certainly an extremely fancy *bar mitzvah*; it is difficult to imagine a more costly and impressive *bar mitzvah*. The actual hall was… well, luxurious. In the center of each table stood an ornate candlestick with a lit candle at its center and a crown of white flowers surrounding it. Everything seemed to sparkle, and Elimelech sat at the center, at the head table, which had been placed on a high platform. Elimelech was beaming with delight. A four piece band completed the

magnificent décor. As they struck up a lively tune, Elimelech was hoisted up on someone's shoulders and the dancing began. It was a very joyous event.

I must tell you that throughout the actual *bar mitzvah* I did not feel, and I do not believe that my friends felt, any resentment or jealousy at all. Quite the opposite: the beauty and the decoration – and of course the joy – drew us all in. We were too busy having a good time to feel jealous.

The problem only began one day later, but let's not jump ahead.

The next morning, learning began later than usual. Elimelech showed up even later still and was welcomed like a victorious general draped in praise returning from the battlefield.

We all gathered around him and listened eagerly as he described the logistics of the previous night's celebration: He told us how many people attended, the gifts they brought, the beautiful set of *Rambam* he received from his grandfather, the respectable sum of money that he received from his mother's brother who traveled to Israel from Manchester especially for his *bar mitzvah*, and on and on.

At a certain point, I happened to turn my head around. That was when I noticed him. Dudi, I mean. He was standing around with the rest of us and was listening carefully to the astonishing descriptions of Elimelech's *bar mitzvah*, but his face appeared sad and pained. It did not take a prophet to tell me what he was feeling; in that brief moment I entered his thoughts and I suddenly felt quite bad myself...

After all, we were celebrating the *bar mitzvah* of Dudi that night. It would have been natural if this fact would have earned him a healthy dose of attention from the boys in our grade. At the moment, however, no one in the class was interested in Dudi or his *bar mitzvah*. We were all firmly under the powerful spell of Elimelech's magnificent *bar mitzvah*.

Dudi's face betrayed his feelings. If his birthday would have preceded Elimelech's by just one night, everything would be so very different. The entire grade would rejoice with him without comparing his celebration to someone else's. Now, however, Elimelech's splendid *bar mitzvah* was set to entirely overshadow his own event...

What should have been Dudi's long-awaited special day of celebration was instantly transformed – for completely external reasons – into a day filled with tension and worry over the upcoming event. I have no doubt that these thoughts were racing through his mind: What will my friends say when they enter the women's section of the *shul* tonight for my *bar mitzvah*? Will they even be happy for me like they were for Elimelech?

I felt a pinch in my heart. For a moment, I wanted to try and steer the class conversation away from Elimelech's *bar mitzvah* and onto another topic. But I realized that Elimelech would feel slighted; he would interpret it as a lack of respect on my part.

I desperately wanted to help Dudi. On the other hand, Elimelech could not be faulted just because his parents made him a lavish *bar mitzvah*. It would not be right to lessen his happiness any more than anyone else's.

• • •

Dudi's *bar mitzvah* was certainly less glamorous – a slight understatement – than Elimelech's. Truth be told, there was nothing wrong with it and it was nothing less than every other *bar mitzvah* in our community. At the same time, it could not possibly compare to the previous night's luxury event.

Throughout the evening, Dudi smiled constantly at everyone and we, his classmates, tried to rejoice and make him happy. But the great differences between the two celebrations held less than twenty-four hours apart seemed to hover over the atmosphere like a heavy cloud.

Yoki could not hold himself in and raised the topic while the *bar mitzvah* meal was still underway. "There's no comparison! This women's section is simply not a celebration hall!" he blurted out in response to Azriel the caterer setting down a large tray on the table and asking each of us in turn, "Potato or vegetable knish?"

Elimelech, who sat just two seats away from Yoki, swallowed a small smile.

"Well, what do you want?" responded Chaim. "Dudi's father does not own a factory."

This time, Elimelech made as if he did not hear.

"Guys, don't you think we should wait until it's over to have this debate?" Nachum whispered loudly.

"You're right," admitted an embarrassed Yoki.

After the celebration ended and we had left the building, the debate continued. Once again it was Yoki who set it all in motion. "It's about time our community had its own celebration hall worthy of its name," he complained.

"A celebration hall is wonderful," pointed out Itzik, "but until such a facility actually exists I think that everyone should be making their *bar mitzvah* in more or less an equal way." This was a slight criticism of Elimelech, but then again, Itzik is the type of boy to say exactly what he thinks.

"That's right," I joined the discussion, "large differences between individuals often produce jealousy and disputes."

Elimelech began protecting the right of each person to lead his life according to his personal means. "It was the Russian communist approach that demanded absolute equality, and that everyone lead identical lifestyles. That approach has long gone out the window!"

"Come on, guys, let's not forget that we are all preparing for our own *bar mitzvo*s that will be held in the *shul* or in the school assembly hall," Nachum reminded us all. Somehow, Nachum always knows how to be the voice of reason in our class debates.

"Correct," and "You're right," came the sound of approval from all sides.

"The way I see it," continued Nachum, meriting the rare attention of the entire grade, "certainly anyone has the right to hold a lavish celebration. But we have to always remember what the 'normal' standard is – and recognize that which is exceptional. In our neighborhood, it is normal to hold a *bar mitzvah* in the *shul* or school. Anyone who does otherwise is exceptional."

Nachum was known for his sharp tongue. Since he was not the type to make arguments, he looked straight at Elimelech and added, "Please don't take this personally, Elimelech. It's just that I think we sort of lost proportion a bit with this whole event..."

It seemed as though the debate had been settled, but the coming days proved otherwise. The discussion grew larger and louder until it became somewhat out of control. The grade quickly found itself divided into two groups, which I refer to as Elimelech's supporters and Nachum's supporters.

As could be expected, those who joined Elimelech's supporters were from the more financially comfortable families. For that reason, I was extremely surprised to discover Kubi among them. Kubi is one of the brightest boys in our grade, but he is the last that I would expect to justify extravagant, flashy displays. One did not need to see Kubi's father's paycheck to know that his family did not suffer from an overabundance of wealth – Kubi practically never wore a new piece of clothing and was never seen with a penny of allowance.

Kubi surprised me not only by the position he took but also by the interesting argument he made. He said, "If the Creator decided to bless a Jew with wealth, then what would you prefer that he spend it on? A fancy car? Clothing? On nonsense? That is exactly why Hashem gave a Jew money – to buy a top-grade pair of *tefillin*, the highest quality *esrog*, and to make a grand and beautiful *bar mitzvah*!"

The debate would not quiet down. The next in line for a *bar mitzvah* was Meni, who had already informed us that his celebration might not take place within our neighborhood.

Meni is an exception because he actually lives outside our neighborhood. Nevertheless, after hearing his announcement, other voices in the class began suggesting that they may also hold their *bar mitzvah* celebrations in a hall outside the community.

Following a solid week of arguments on this issue, the commotion reached the ears of the teacher we all admire, Rabbi Levin. He decided to devote an entire afternoon, as he put it – to "clarify the debate, examining it from all sides."

First, Rabbi Levin allowed each boy to express his own view. He noted that in addition to tackling the current hot topic, it was equally important to train ourselves to listen to the various views among us, whether we agreed with them or not. In truth, this was a powerful lesson in conducting a debate with a large number of participants in a dignified and respectful manner.

When we were all done, it was Rabbi Levin's turn to summarize all that had been said and then to express his own opinion. We were intensely curious to discover what *he* thought about the great *bar mitzvah* debate.

"Dear students," he began, "it may seem that I only became aware of the class dispute today. In fact, I was informed about it the morning after Dudi's *bar mitzvah.* A number of parents told me about the argument that had developed. They asked me to intervene, explaining that it would be extremely sad to turn such an important year – a year in which you enter the age of performing *mitzvos* and prepare to enter *yeshivah* – into a year of arguments and debates. At first, however, I deliberately allowed you to argue among yourselves for a few days..."

Rabbi Levin looked at us kindly before continuing, "There is another angle here to which you have failed to pay attention – and that is precisely what I wish to focus on. You have all been discussing concepts of money, social gaps, and jealousy between students. But have any of you ever questioned – 'What is a *bar mitzvah* altogether?' How are we to understand that just a moment earlier I was a playful boy and now I have suddenly become a 'man' who is obligated in all of the *mitzvos* of the Torah? Has even one of you considered that on the day of his *bar mitzvah*, he and Moshe *Rabbeinu* are perfectly equal in regards to completing a *minyan*?"

Rabbi Levin gave a light cough and continued, "When you consider this, then what importance can you give to the size of the hall or the quality of the food at a *bar mitzvah* celebration?"

He continued holding us spellbound with his enlightening words. I felt him opening my eyes and completely changing my attitude towards a *bar mitzvah*.

The real surprise was kept for last. Approximately half an hour before the end of the school day, Rabbi Levin peered at his watch and announced, "I have invited a special guest here today, who would like to address you."

Rabbi Levin gave a mysterious smile and we just looked at each other in surprise and with great curiosity. Who on earth could he be referring to?

Our teacher then approached the classroom door and opened it ever so slightly. A moment later, he flung it wide open and with a motion of his hand, invited an unseen figure to enter the room.

• • •

The most unexpected person walked into our classroom.

We were all taken by surprise, but the greatest shock belonged to Elimelech – "the tall." He gazed at his father with ever-increasing astonishment. His father rapidly glanced around the classroom and when he noticed his son, he gave a slightly embarrassed smile that was at the same time gently reassuring.

I tried to guess what Elimelech's father intended to tell us. Does he want to rebuke us for our attitude towards his son, I wondered? I immediately pushed that thought away. It was illogical to assume that he would come here for that, and even more illogical to assume that Rabbi Levin would permit him to do so. Especially while Rabbi Levin was attempting to settle our agitated debate once and for all.

Rabbi Levin sat on the chair that stood permanently beside the classroom door, and Elimelech's father took the teacher's place at the front desk.

"I would like to tell you a story," Elimelech's father began. "This is a true story that occurred many years ago."

I glanced once more at Elimelech; he sat there looking tense.

"Sixty years ago, a couple in their early thirties immigrated to Israel from Western Europe. Although they had been married for a number of years by that time, they did not have any children.

"At first, they lived in a *mabarah*, a transit camp for new arrivals to the country, which was located next to Haifa. Such camps consisted of cabins and tents and were created in order to absorb the waves of immigrants reaching the shores of Israel from North Africa and Europe.

"The husband worked at paving streets, picking citrus fruits, and similar exhausting manual labor. At the end of each month, he would collect a few measly pennies on which he and his wife were forced to survive throughout the coming month. Two years after their arrival in Israel, the government gave them an old, tiny house in northern Tel Aviv. Despite their difficulties, they were always happy with what they had and looked forward to a brighter future.

"In Tel Aviv, they were blessed their first – and only – child. Their delight knew no bounds. They adored the little boy with all their heart and watched over him like hawks. They made do with minimal food in order to provide their son with adequate food and clothing. Once the child began attending school, they would accompany him each morning to class. In the afternoon, after the school day had ended, the mother would go out to meet and greet her son.

"Sometimes, during late *Shabbos* afternoons, they would stroll along the streets of (what was then small) Tel Aviv, clutching the hands of their precious child. The boy was their pride and joy. Their every challenge seemed insignificant compared to this great gift.

"One day, when their cherished son was in fifth grade, their delight was abruptly severed.

"It was towards evening on a dark, cloudy day. The mother followed her daily routine of meeting her son on his way back from school. That evening, when the son saw his mother approaching, he got ready to run across the road that separated them.

"At that precise moment, a car emerged from around the bend in the street and the mother, who noticed it speeding their way, acted quickly to prevent an accident. She realized that her son had not seen the vehicle speeding towards him and was about to dash across the road, right in its path. Making a split second decision, she began running towards him, intending to reach

him before he set foot in the road – stopping him from running towards her.

"It was clear that she thought she had enough time to reach him before the car reached that spot. Perhaps the thought of her dear son's life in danger confused her thinking. The car's impact was fatal. She indeed saved her son's life, but paid for it with her own.

"In an instant, the bliss that had enveloped the family shattered into a thousand fragments. The boy was left orphaned from his mother and found himself completely alone in his father's world. His father took the tragedy extremely hard; he was irreversibly heartbroken. At first, he tried his hardest to raise his son alone, but it soon became impossible. His work demanded that he be absent from the house much of the time; there was no one to look after the child.

"After a year, the father came to the realization that there was no choice but to send his son to a boarding school. At the age of eleven, the boy traveled to a boarding school in the north of the country. There he was raised and educated, while having to cope with the many difficult challenges of a boarding school life.

"After two years, he reached the age of *bar mitzvah*. Well, you can only imagine what sort of *bar mitzvah* he had. It was a modest celebration, held within the confines of the boarding school, without a mother or any other relatives – except for his father who traveled from Tel Aviv by bus. One can say with certainty that it was an extremely miserable *bar mitzvah*.

"Many years passed. The boy grew up and with Hashem's help merited to raise a family of his own and succeeded in supporting his family very comfortably. He had a number of children and raised them gratefully. But he never forgot his humble and painful roots. He never desired to live a life of extravagance and waste.

"When his eldest son reached the age of *bar mitzvah*, he felt a strong personal need to compensate in some way for his own miserable *bar mitzvah*. For that reason, he decided to arrange a most lavish *bar mitzvah* for his son. He told himself, 'I will give my son the happiness that I never had.'"

Elimelech's father paused in his speech to look at his son, as if requesting permission to continue.

"If you haven't guessed until now… the boy who was orphaned from his mother at a young age and who grew up in a boarding school – was me."

He bit his lower lip and continued, "And so, dear children, I have not come here today to confess before you… I came to give you a message. In fact, a number of messages:

"Firstly, it is important to remember that often, when we see someone else's life sparkling – that's just one part of the total picture. We tend to be jealous of others, but that happens because we see only the light glittering in their lives and not the dark shadows. Believe me, there is not a person on earth whose entire life is light, without shadows...

"Secondly, parents sometimes make certain decisions in regards to their children, only in order to fill voids that they – the parents – carry in their hearts from their own youth. I am not at all certain that this is the best or correct thing to do, but when we look at it within this context – everything looks very different.

"Over the course of the last few weeks, I have been closely following – with the help of my discussions with Elimelech – what was going on in the grade. What can I tell you? My heart aches. The bottom line is that I deeply regret making such an extravagant *bar mitzvah* for Elimelech, and also for holding it outside the neighborhood. But the *bar mitzvah* has passed and my regret will not accomplish anything. I thought to myself that perhaps if I were to tell you my story, perhaps we could derive something positive from this whole affair..."

The story of Elimelech's father was both moving and heartrending. It was astounding to observe how an event that seemed to convey one impression could convey, in just a moment, an entirely different meaning. That is, only if we look at it with the proper perspective.

An Inheritance Worth Millions

One of the characteristics of our charming neighborhood is routine. Some claim that routine brings blessing; others insist that it makes things dull. My father, for example, is an avid fan of routine. He is an admirably orderly and organized person, who does not appreciate surprises in life.

When he is asked, "How are thing?" he replies, "*Boruch Hashem*, I have a routine." He explains with a smile that the Chinese have a curse, "May you have an interesting life..." It is not a good sign – so he claims – when things are too interesting.

I, however (if I am permitted to differ, with all due respect to my father), think that a life devoid of routine-shattering events is – how should I put it? Somewhat boring.

Whichever way you want to look at it, a result of the routine that dominates our neighborhood is that each event that indeed manages to shake its residents, or at least a few of them, from the boredom of daily life, merits excessive attention. Events are discussed weeks before their due date and they remain the source of local chatter long after they have ended.

It was little wonder, then, that when signs were posted in our neighborhood this week – proclaiming an event that is scheduled to take place in our community in ten days time – it immediately generated a storm of widespread interest. The fact that from all the residents, it was specifically Reb Daniel who signed these announcements, greatly enhanced public curiosity.

Reb Daniel is a quiet man, whose voice is hardly heard. Someone once joked that it was not by chance that Reb Daniel's family name is Sol (as in the name of the fish, "sole") – the appearance Reb Daniel projected was of an eternally calm man with a beaming, content face, who swims gently through the currents of life. Anyone who knows Reb Daniel, however, is aware that he does not have an easy life at all. Hashem has blessed him with a large family, but an extremely meager livelihood.

Reb Daniel serves as a *menaker* in a fresh chicken factory. A *menaker* is one whose job it is to extract the parts of *shechted* chickens or cows that we are forbidden to eat according to *Halachah*. It requires a trained expert and great precision, and Reb Daniel performs this work throughout the night. It is not an easy job, nor does it bring much in the way of a salary.

Around half a year ago, Reb Daniel's father passed away. He had lived in a town in New Jersey, in the United States, and was what people call "a traditional Jew." He passed away on a Friday and the news reached his son in Israel just a short while before *Shabbos*.

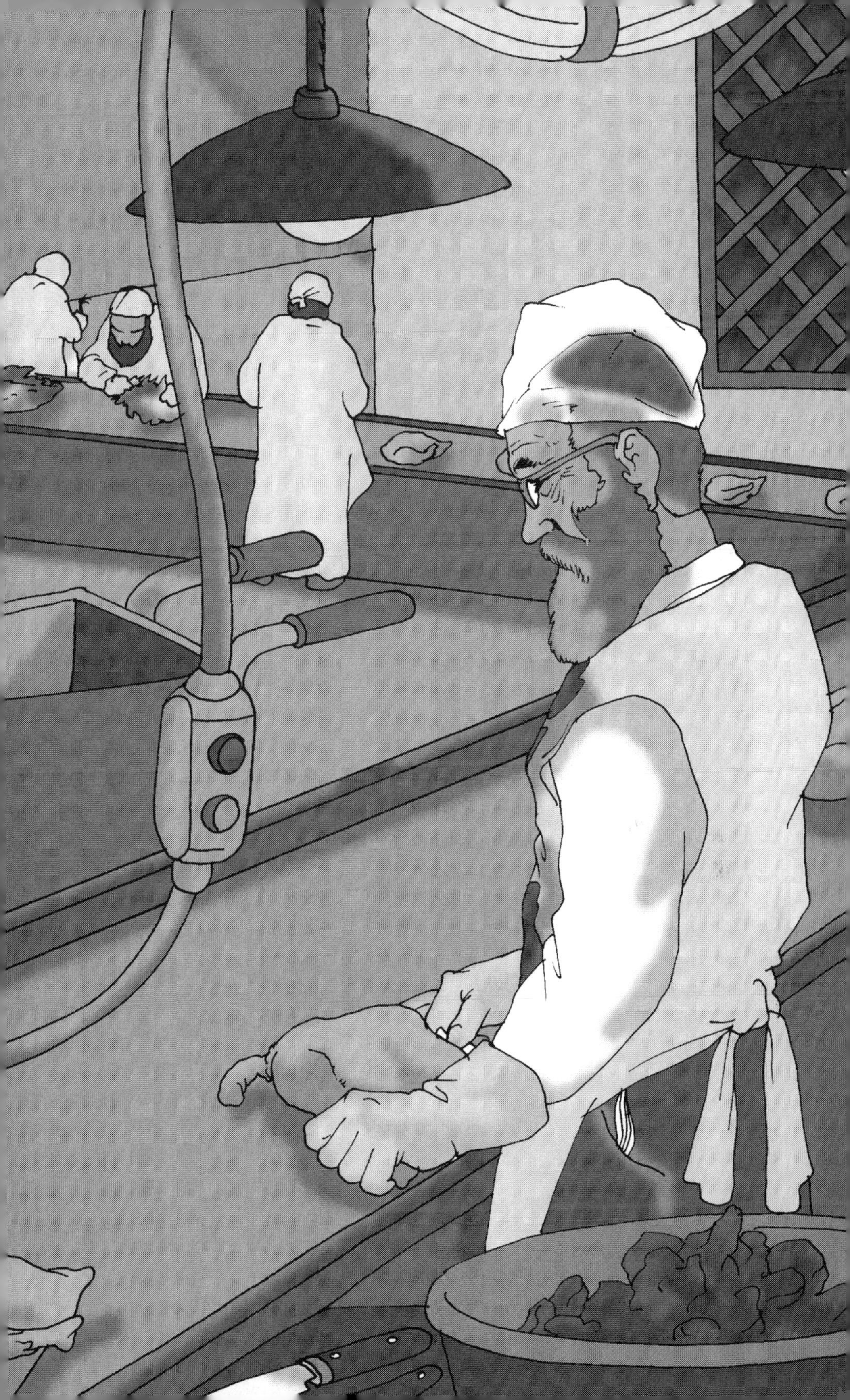

Our community rabbi decided that it would be incorrect to have the body of his father remain unburied for two days until Reb Daniel could arrive from Israel. Rather, effort must be made to have him buried immediately, before the onset of *Shabbos* in the United States. The Rabbi advised Reb Daniel to remain in Israel and sit *shiva* (the seven days of mourning) where he is. After all, his mother had already passed away years before and he had no brothers. His closest family and friends were all located in Israel.

You must be wondering why I am burdening you with all these details. What does this have to do with an upcoming event that has the whole community talking? Well, stick with me and you can be certain that everything will make sense in the end...

Reb Daniel followed our Rabbi's advice and observed *shiva* in his own home. He did not fly to the United States even after the seven days were over. He said that he might make the trip to New York at the conclusion of the entire year of mourning in order to visit the graves of his parents.

Nevertheless, just two months after his father's passing, Reb Daniel flew out of the country. As usual, he did not say much about it. Even his handful of closest friends did not receive any clear information about the purpose of his trip. Despite that, someone claimed that Reb Daniel had whispered to him on the night before departing that "the purpose of this trip justifies all of the time and effort that was put in..."

Various rumors and guesses began to circulate. At the center of it all was a key word that was heard time and time again and seemed to fuel the ceaseless speculation – "Inheritance."

To give you a better idea, here is a basic summary of the main rumors: Reb Daniel's father was a prominent and successful businessman. He dealt in real estate, with diamonds, or in the food industry (this has not been entirely clarified as of yet). Throughout his life, he consistently refused to provide financial support for his only son because he was aggravated by his son having become *frum* as a teenager, who then immigrated to Israel and enrolled in a *yeshivah*. Now that he had passed away, however, there was nothing to prevent the transfer of an inheritance worth millions into the bank account of Reb Daniel – according to the rumors, that is.

The thought that a new millionaire (okay, the only millionaire…) had joined our neighborhood set the imagination of its residents racing. In addition, the concept of a sudden meeting between riches and Reb Daniel amused them tremendously.

"Reb Daniel? A millionaire? Why, he would have a hard time recognizing a coin if he met one!" I overheard one of Reb Dovid's sons-in-law telling him. "Well, maybe we will begin to involve him in the business," responded Reb Dovid in a way that may have been teasing or may have been serious.

Naturally, this quickly became the source of discussion in our grade. We tried to imagine the impact of newfound wealth on the life of Reb Daniel.

"He will finally exchange his worn out jacket for a new one," laughed Yoki.

"We may also see him traveling in some expensive car," added Dudi. The very idea generated peals of laughter.

"Expensive, you say?" smirked Itzik, "I've never even seen him enter a banged up Beetle!"

I should really point out that at home we would never have held such a discussion.

"It is none of our business to inquire into the personal lives of others," my father responded forcefully when I once merely mentioned the name of Reb Daniel. "It falls under the Torah's prohibition of *rechilus* – spreading rumors."

My mother confirmed that she thought likewise, "In the end, such talk always evolves into *lashon hara* – slander."

A few weeks later, the news spread like wildfire: "He's back!" No one needed to explain who "he" was or from where "he" returned. Evidently, Reb Daniel had arrived back from his trip to New Jersey.

"Well?" Chaim teased Yoki, "you told us that he might finally change his old jacket, didn't you? Forget about it! I saw him this morning. What a jacket… not a thing has changed."

There was a sense of disappointment, but the intriguing mystery still hovered in the air – did he or did he not receive an inheritance? Or to put in more bluntly – was he now a millionaire or not?

Reb Daniel continued to maintain his usual air of silence, completely disregarding all questions or hints directed his way.

Around three months after Reb Daniel's return to Israel, notices appeared in the community.

To most people, the announcement seemed to confirm all of the guesswork and gossip regarding Reb Daniel's inheritance. It appears, people told each other, that Reb Daniel has decided not to make a fuss about his wealth in the manner of many who gain significant sums of money quite unexpectedly; for that reason, he has not altered one iota of his previous lifestyle. It also appears that he has chosen to invest his first use of the riches in a sacred cause – having a *sefer* Torah written and presented to the *shul* in memory of his late father.

Not everyone is capable of financing a Torah and especially not with such short notice. Then again, what does forty or fifty thousand dollars mean to a millionaire like Reb Daniel...

• • •

Sisu ve-simchu be-simchas Torah, u-senu kavod la-Torah, screamed the headlines on the modest printed posters. "Rejoice in the celebration of the Torah! Give honor to the Torah!"

We are pleased to inform you of the welcoming of a new Torah to our *shul* in the merit of the late Reb Shimon ben Reb Daniel, of blessed memory, from New Jersey, who departed this world with a sterling reputation.

The community is hereby invited to the ceremony of inscribing the final letters in the Torah that will be held in the home of the Sol family on Thursday, the 12th of *Sivan*.

Following the ceremony, the new scroll will be escorted through the streets to the *shul* with large crowds and great fanfare.

With blessings in honor of the new Torah,

– The *Gabbaim* and the Sol Family

Despite the considerable effort to resolve the rumors buzzing around Reb Daniel's supposed inheritance, the Torah welcoming ceremony was exceptionally moving and uplifting. The entire neighborhood was swept up in the happy event; the joy was great and palpable. At the center of the festivities stood Reb Daniel, who appeared to be in seventh heaven. He danced and sang energetically with the Torah in his hands to the point that it was difficult to imagine that this was the same Reb Daniel who remained extraordinarily silent and discreet all these many years.

Our class was appointed to watch over the boys of the lower grades who marched behind the Torah's *chupah* with lit torches in their hands.

When the parade arrived at the *shul*, we recited the verses of *Atah Horesa*, following which the new Torah was entered into the *aron kodesh* with much singing and dancing. The community then sat down for a *seudas mitzvah* – celebratory meal that provided plenty of food and refreshments, during the course of which the main star of the celebration – Reb Daniel – was honored with an opportunity to address the crowd. This was the moment, in my humble estimation, for which many were waiting.

Reb Daniel approached the microphone and bashfully lowered his eyes. It seemed that he had not yet come to terms with the fact that he was at the center of such a festive and well-attended event.

"*She-hechiyanu ve-kimanu ve-higi'anu la-zman ha-zeh* – I Thank Hashem for allowing us to reach such an auspicious occasion!" he began with deep emotion discernable in his voice. "It is not every day that one merits to donate a new Torah to the *shul*, and

especially not a Torah such as this that carries a unique family story..."

"See," whispered my friend Nachum, "the secret about the inheritance is about to be lifted..."

"Friends, please allow me to share the story of this scroll with you," Reb Daniel continued.

"Certainly! Please do!" someone called out (perhaps overly) enthusiastically from the crowd.

"It all began right before the outbreak of the Second World War," explained Reb Daniel. The assembled were instantly hushed. "My grandfather, for whom I am named – Reb Daniel Solberg of blessed memory – then lived in a small Belgium village containing just ten or so Jewish families. Nevertheless, my grandfather maintained a small *shul* that housed a Torah, which he had paid to have written.

"When war broke out and the Germans threatened to conquer large areas of Europe including Belgium (which was in fact rapidly conquered shortly after), my grandfather realized that if he wished to survive, it would be best to leave the country at the first opportunity. Due to the circumstances of the time, he decided to hide his Torah scroll for safekeeping in the local medical center run by the monastery. He knew that it would remain protected there for the duration of the war.

"'One day, I will return and collect it,' he assured the nuns.

"He and his family fled from Belgium and settled in the United States. A few years later, my grandfather passed away and his Torah scroll was all but forgotten.

"My late father grew up and opened a factory for recycling paper; he was extremely successful in his business. Unfortunately, he drifted away from the Torah life with which he was raised in his father's home, but he was not detached entirely. In my youth, I was sent to a religious summer camp and it lit a spark within me. As the years went by, I grew increasingly drawn to Torah and *mitzvos*. When most of my friends enrolled in various universities, my heart told me that my place was in a *yeshivah* – and not just any *yeshivah*, but specifically one that was located in the Holy Land. This move greatly upset my father and mother.

"Many years passed. Then, around eleven years ago, my father desired to fly from the United States to Belgium in order to trace his roots. He was not that young anymore and since I was his only son, he requested that I accompany him on his trip to Belgium. I honored his wishes.

"During this trip, which lasted around ten days, my father and I struck up a new relationship with each other. He began to show more understanding of my lifestyle.

"Something else, equally important, occurred during the trip – and that is what I would like to tell you:

"On the second day of our stay in Belgium, we searched for the address at which my father had lived throughout his infancy and childhood, until the war. As we were still standing there eagerly examining the building, a neighbor happened to look out of his window. He was an elderly man, but despite his age a keen alertness sparkled in his eyes.

"'Who are you?' he questioned. My father identified himself, and the elderly man grew enormously emotional. 'So you are the son of Daniel Solberg!' he cried in disbelief. 'We were very close friends. Why, I even have some photographs of you...'

"The man invited us into his home and showed us the photographs. He explained that he used to work as a photographer. His collection included images of my father in his youth, which was a truly wonderful surprise. He handed the pictures to my father, adding, 'You were very lucky to have come here today; I am leaving my home tomorrow permanently for a senior center.'

"Before we left, the gentleman requested my father's phone number in the United States as well as my phone number in Israel.

"As I said, that was eleven years ago. Then, just two months ago, I received a phone call from that elderly man; he was still alive and his mind was perfectly clear.

"'I have some information that will interest you,' he announced. 'Are you aware that your grandfather hid a Torah scroll in the local monastery's medical center? Well, a few weeks ago, the floor of the attic in the ancient medical center was ripped out. Among the items discovered there was your grandfather's Torah. I would never have known about it were it not for a small notice in the local newspaper that I read cover to cover each morning. According to the information provided, a nun reported that one of the elderly sisters had passed away a few years ago; before she died, she had informed her colleagues that a Jew named Solberg hid a Torah scroll for safekeeping in the attic shortly before the war. The advisory concluded with a request: "Does anyone have any information about the owner the scroll, or his descendants?" Now, as I explained to your father, I knew your grandfather and grandmother extremely well. And thanks to your visit here a few years back, I was able to reach you.'

"'The elderly Belgian hesitated and then added questioningly, 'I have been trying to reach your father for two weeks now, without success. I assume that he has changed his address?'

"'Yes,' I replied, 'He has certainly relocated...' When I elaborated, the gentleman expressed his deep sorrow.

"In short, I was invited to Belgium to reclaim my grandfather's Torah scroll. And therefore..."

At this point, Reb Daniel tried to suppress a small smile before continuing.

"For the information of all those who are particularly interested: When I was absent from the neighborhood recently, I was in fact staying in Belgium and not New Jersey. When I returned, I brought with me a truly priceless treasure: the Torah scroll that had been commissioned by my grandfather and which had finally merited to be redeemed from its lengthy captivity and restored to its natural location – the *shul's aron kodesh*."

Having ended his speech, Reb Daniel returned to his place at one of the tables.

It was easy to discern the amazement written over the faces of many of those present. The rumors of an inheritance had not been upheld. On the other hand, it seemed that Reb Daniel had managed, with the aid of his moving story, to redirect the burning curiosity based on pure gossip as to whether or not he had become a billionaire – to a more truthful and serious fact.

In his own words: "I brought with me a truly priceless treasure..."

The Grand Trip

Two months before the end of the school year, we enjoyed our annual grand trip. This year, it was also our final trip as students of the *cheder* before entering the *yeshivah* system.

The students of each grade in *cheder* wait impatiently all year for the annual trip. First of all, these events are always long and filled with exciting experiences. Secondly, and perhaps most importantly, the person in charge of all trips in our school is none other than our principal, Rabbi Shiyeh.

Rabbi Shiyeh is a complicated character. On one hand, he is a goodhearted person. On *Shabbos*, he is everyone's friendly uncle. He distributes candy to all the children in the *shul*. In school, however, he is the overly strict type. It is simply not worth tangling with him.

When Rabbi Shiyeh fixes you with his two penetrating eyes, you feel entirely transparent. When he asks you something, it does not even enter your mind to sell him a fake story.

Rabbi Shiyeh is not a dramatic person; he does not use fancy speech at all. The opposite is true. Nevertheless, when he gives you a piercing look and utters a sarcastic sentence such as, "it seems that you insist that we invite your parents here so they can derive some "*nachas*" from you…" – his words seem to cut deeply into your flesh.

Things reach a climax when Rabbi Shiyeh knocks on the door of a classroom in the middle of a class and enters. He has a very distinctive knock (two short and rapid raps). When we hear that sound at our door, we know that there is trouble brewing. A student had acted violently. Something in the classroom had been destroyed. Someone in the neighborhood had complained about the inappropriate conduct of one of the students...

What about Rabbi Shiyeh's punishments? You can never predict them in advance.

Once, for example, one of the students in the *cheder* was caught picking grapefruit from the private grapefruit tree of Yom Tov the Watchmaker (see – our community even has its own watchmaker…). The principal had the student work in the school's garden during every recess for an entire week.

"Perhaps after working hard and sweating a little in order to grow things from the ground, you might learn to appreciate a tree that someone else nurtured and grew with the toil of their hands," he told the astounded boy.

Nevertheless, the fear that Rabbi Shiyeh instills into the students on an average school day is matched by an equally great friendship and openness that Rabbi Shiyeh displays towards each student during the annual trips. Then, it seems, he permits the image of a stern principal to slip away, revealing a warm human hidden within.

During the trips, Rabbi Shiyeh shines. He walks between the students as if he was the patriarch of a large family enjoying his many descendants. He gives a friendly tweak of the cheek, compliments when he sees things in order or particularly good conduct. He will approach a group of children who have found themselves a quiet corner and play a game with them.

My friend Nachum claims that both the severity and softness of Rabbi Shiyeh stem from the fact that he does not have any children of his own. It is sad to see that the hair of Rabbi Shiyeh has long turned white, but he and his wife have not been blessed with children.

At first, Nachum's words sounded strange and absurd to me. But the more I think about it, the more I believe he may be correct. What do *you* think about it?

Let us leave that topic for a moment and return to our discussion of the grand trips.

Rabbi Shiyeh is a thorough person. The annual trips are arranged in a most efficient and organized way. On top of that, he is a true expert in everything connected with the Land of Israel. He once told us that he gained his knowledge of the land through his feet – he had toured it extensively by foot over many years. During the actual trip, it is fantastic to observe his outstanding familiarity with every location and thing that we encounter. He is a walking encyclopedia.

That's the way he is with the trips for every class. You can only imagine what he is like when it comes to the grand trip for the oldest class in *cheder*. The trip lasts for a number of days and includes tents and camp equipment. The annual trip at the conclusion of the eighth grade has become a legend that is transmitted from one generation to the next in our school.

This year, Rabbi Shiyeh decided to take us to the Golan Heights, with the intention of placing emphasis on the ancient *shuls* in that area. I do not know how exciting that sounds to you, but now that the trip is over, I can tell you with absolute certainly that it was unbelievable. The blend of green landscapes and flowers, streams and vibrant waterfalls, magnificent observation points and a personal meeting with our people's ancient history. All of this was enhanced by the detailed explanations of our principal, creating an unforgettable experience.

There was also something else that made this particular trip impossible to forget.

It happened on the first day of the trip.

At first, everything proceeded according to plan. The path we followed that day was in an area called Nachal Gilbon (the Gilbon/Jilabun Stream) at the heart of the Golan Heights, to the north of Katzrin. We traveled there in four jeeps that bounced over cleared paths, and arrived at a wide clearing from which we began our hike along an hour-long trail.

Along the way, we encountered the remains of Syrian villages that had been abandoned after the Six Day War. We set off on a trail that twisted its way between thick eucalyptus trees and came to the banks of a river that flowed non-stop throughout the year. We trekked in the shade and sang beautiful songs. We marched in unity until we reached a spectacular observation point. From there, a path led off towards the ancient village of Devorah. We climbed up to the highest point in the village and gazed at the breathtaking scenery spread out before us – the Hula Valley.

"Come," Rabbi Shiyeh suddenly announced as he waved us forward with his hand. "I want to show you something..." He began striding towards a path that led us to the remains of an Arab village called Daburiah. "This was once the location of an ancient Jewish village that flourished in the times of the *Mishneh* and *Gemara*. Around a hundred years ago, a Bedouin tribe called Naarneh arrived here and they used the stones that remained from the ancient Jewish homes to build their own houses.

"After the Six Day War, an ancient stone tablet bearing Hebrew inscription was discovered. The Bedouin had used it as a lintel over a doorway in one of their homes, but it was later discovered by experts who revealed that it had once formed part of the carved inscription that formed the lintel of the *shul* of the ancient *tanna*, Rabbi Eliezer *Hakapar* – he was one of the colleagues of Rabbi Yehudah *Hanasi*. Because of its great historic value, the stone was removed from here and entrusted to the Israel Museum."

The principal paused for a while and a slight smile formed at the corners of his eyes. "Now let me ask you a question. Whoever knows the answer will receive a special reward from me later on." Rabbi Shiyeh is an avid fan of Torah trivia riddles.

"Who knows how many times Rabbi Eliezer *Hakapar* is mentioned throughout the entire *Mishneh*?"

We racked our brains trying to think of any lesson in which we recall hearing the name of Rabbi Eliezer.

The voice of Meni Feinberg cut through the silence, "I am not certain how many times he is mentioned in the *Mishneh*, but I do remember his teaching in *Pirkei Avos*."

"And what is it?" questioned the principal.

"'Jealousy, lust, and honor drive a person from the world,'" Meni replied.

"Excellent!" beamed Rabbi Shiyeh. "You should know that the *Mishneh* in *Avos* is the only time that Rabbi Elizer Hakapar is mentioned in the entire series of *Mishneh*." The principal promised Meni the reward.

Rabbi Shiyeh led us around the structure and showed us another stone approximately one meter long. An image of an eagle holding a wreath in its beak and with two fish at its side was carved into the stone.

"Some claim that this stone was part of the *shul* in the Jewish settlement here," explained Rabbi Shiyeh.

He then took us to the edge of the ruined village and showed us the remains of olive oil presses. "It appears that this was the primary source of income for the residents of the ancient village."

I had a good look at all these things, touched the ancient rocks, and felt moved. I was experiencing history.

• • •

It was afternoon, and the sun blazed down at us. It was a good thing that we all had caps and water bottles. We left the ancient Jewish village and trekked after Rabbi Shiyeh along a path marked by blue paint. Our destination was the Devorah Waterfall.

Treading with great care, we moved along a path that brought us under the thirty foot high waterfall. The descent was somewhat steep and we held onto iron pegs that had been fixed into the rocks. At the bottom of the path, we found ourselves next to a plunge pool into which the water cascaded. We removed our shoes and socks and splashed our feet in the cool waters. Some brave boys jumped into the pool with their clothes on and began splashing around. Rabbi Shiyeh and our two teachers (Rabbi Levin and Rabbi Rosen) glanced at each other and smiled with satisfaction. Within a few minutes we were all in the water. We swam, sent water flying in every direction, and had a really good time.

We left the pool, dried ourselves out in the hot sun, and then sat in a shady spot to eat lunch, surrounded by a sea of colorful flowering.

"Perhaps, Chaim, you wouldn't mind explaining a little about the colorful blooms all around us?" asked the principal. As I mentioned previously, Rabbi Shiyeh is a completely different person during these trips. He tries to pay individual attention to each child.

All eyes turned to look at Chaim, who blushed. He eventually overcame his shyness and stood up. He began a short and educational speech, pointing toward various clumps of vegetation that sprouted around us.

"Over there is oleander," he announced, pointing towards a mass of delicate pink flowers. "And those are raspberries," he added, stepping towards clusters of small red berries dangling at the center of a thorny shrub. "Now, there – look over there," continued Chaim with impressive expertise, "you are able to see a plant with a very interesting name. The plant is called Abraham's Balm. What does it have to do with our patriarch Avraham? Well, the botanists who provided it with a name decided that this is the precise species of shrub in whose branches the horns of the ram became entangled while Avraham was preparing to offer his son Yitzchok..."

After the brief lecture on the world of plants, Rabbi Rosen told us a beautiful story with a good lesson that involves one of the Torah sages. We recited *birchas hamozon* and stood up to continue our hike.

It was now five in the afternoon. Rabbi Shiyeh and the two teachers had a short discussion between themselves regarding the timing schedule. "I arranged with the jeep drivers to wait for us next to the Gilbon Waterfall," I overheard the principal say. He looked at his watch and declared, "According to the clock, we have plenty of time. There are still another three hours of sunlight. The route to the waterfall will not take more than half an hour. We have time to arrive there, *daven minchah*, enjoy the place a bit, and then travel to our camping grounds at Katzrin – we can do all this before it gets dark."

Once their discussion ended, we set off. "What? We are going to *another* waterfall?" Yoki challenged the principal in a provocative tone. "Wait, wait until we get there," answered Rabbi Shiyeh, "Then you will realize that the small splash of water you experienced here was simply a miniature sample of what a real waterfall looks like..."

Twenty five minutes later, we arrived at the Gilbon Waterfall. Our principal was totally correct. The scene was breathtaking. It was almost one-hundred-fifty feet high. Its waters emerged from the top of a cliff whose walls were made of black basalt rock and it was flanked on either side by thick green vegetation. The waters crashed down with a thunderous roar into the plunge pool beneath, from which the Gilbon Stream flowed away into the distance. We stood around the churning pool with water droplets flying into our faces, refreshing us in the heat of the day.

It was pleasant to *daven minchah* in the heart of nature. The roar of the waterfall, the chirping of birds, and the flowers and plants on every side made it seem as if nature itself was joining our *davening*. After *minchah*, we took pictures with the falls in the background, making all sorts of poses. Many students took pictures of themselves posing with the teachers.

After approximately a quarter of an hour, I noticed a concerned expression on the principal's face. He approached Rabbi Levin and whispered something in his ear. His eyes quickly turned to track down Rabbi Rosen in the distance and the principal approached him as well. A moment later, the cause became clear. "Has anyone seen Elimelech and Shuki?" Rabbi Shiyeh asked with an urgent tone in his voice. Within minutes we were all searching for the missing boys.

I have told you plenty about Elimelech, but not Shuki. Shuki is a friendly and likeable boy, with just one obvious fault. He loves to play mischievous pranks.

Shuki once brought three young chicks in a shoebox to the classroom. During a *Halacha* test he set them free. Another time, he disguised himself as an elderly gentleman and pounded on the classroom door after the class had already begun. It took a few moments to figure out who it really was. That amused us immensely, but the teacher did not take it the same way.

That's Shuki. What is interesting and even surprising is that Elimelech, who is as serious a student as they come, shares a powerful friendship with Shuki. It has happened a number of times that Shuki has persuaded Elimelech to participate in one of his pranks. A psychologist would probably tell you that they are "two entirely opposite personalities that are attracted to their opposites."

We suddenly heard a loud shout that successfully overcame the roaring of the waterfall. “There they are!” It was Meni. He pointed to two tiny figures at the very top of the waterfall.

Rabbi Shiyeh looked upwards and his face suddenly paled. “May they be well, that pair…” he muttered in suppressed anger. He verified that he had an open view of the peak and then began waving with his two raised hands, signaling to Elimelech and Shuki to keep a distance from the edge of the waterfall. It was doubtful indeed whether the boys were actually able to make out his motions from that height, and they most certainly could not understand his intentions.

“You wait here with the students,” Rabbi Shiyeh instructed the two teachers. “I am very familiar with the path. I am going to run up there. Keep the cell phones close to your ears so that you will be able to hear them ring over the sound of the waterfall. I may need to guide you through the cell phone.” With that, he began climbing up a narrow pathway that apparently led to the summit of the cliff.

Shuki and Elimelech had no idea of the worry they were causing us. We then noticed Shuki approach the edge of the cliff and make various movements with his arms, hoping to catch our attention. He seemed to be drawing closer to the edge every second.

And then something terrible happened. Shuki slipped and fell.

We held our breath in horror and then let out a collective cry of fear. Someone flew like lightening after the principal and spoke briefly with him. A second later we saw the principal returning towards us in a frantic dash. He looked upwards and his eyes darkened. Shuki, it seemed, was suspended between heaven and earth. He was tightly holding onto vegetation that emerged from

between the sharp rocks, just a few meters from the edge of the cliff.

• • •

What if the plants snap or give way? What if Shuki's grip begins to weaken? Shuki would slip and fall into the roaring falls beneath his feet. It is difficult to describe the terror that gripped our hearts. We looked at the principal and the teachers in the hope that they would know what to do. Some of my friends could not handle the scene and burst into tears.

The principal seemed to be coming back to himself and was trying to decide the best course of action. It took him just a few seconds and then he whipped a small notepad out of his pocket, scribbled something in it and handed it to Rabbi Levin.

"Call that number," he instructed, "zero-four, six-nine, six-one, eight-four-nine. It's the Golan Heights Rescue Unit. Explain to them what's going on. Ask them to send us a rescue team as quickly as possible."

As Rabbi Levin was dialing, the principal turned to Rabbi Rosen. "You remain standing here and don't remove your eyes from Shuki for even one second."

He then gave us a swift glance. "And all of you…? After me!" he commanded.

Rabbi Shiyeh broke into a run, charging up the same path he had begun to ascend previously. We all charged after him, trying to keep up with his pace. We were surprised at how swiftly he ran. "Everyone, take off your shirts!" he yelled over his shoulder towards us as we drew close to the cliff top. At first, we were not sure that we had heard right. "Take off your shirts!" Rabbi Shiyeh shouted again, "What don't you understand?!"

We continued running. "Every boy must hold his shirt in his hand," Rabbi Shiyeh continued commanding. We began removing our shirts as we ran.

We reached the top of the cliff, close to the waterfall. There was a rock protrusion, a kind of natural balcony, from which we were able to look down to the foot of the waterfall. This was precisely where Elimelech and Shuki had stood just moments before. Now, only Elimelech remained there. He sat on the ground, holding his knees in his hands and trembling like a leaf in the wind.

"From where exactly did Shuki fall?" asked the principal.

Elimelech was not able to utter a sound. He was in shock. With shaking legs, he stood up slowly and took two steps. He pointed toward the spot where he had last seen Shuki.

"Bring me all the shirts!" commanded Rabbi Shiyeh. We handed them to him without understanding why he would want them. Moments later, it all became clear. He started tying the sleeve of one shirt to the sleeve of another in extremely tight knots until he had created a lengthy "rope" out of our shirts.

Rabbi Shiyeh appeared very tense but also extremely focused. "Come – you… you… you…" He pointed to the five tallest and strongest students. "All of you sit down here on the ground and hold this end of the rope with all of your strength."

With the other end of the rope in his hand, Rabbi Shiyeh quickly and carefully approached the edge of the cliff. He lay down flat on the earth, with the upper half of his body protruding over the edge. He could now see Shuki right below him.

He began to speak with Shuki. We could hear him shouting, "Shuki, it's me Rabbi Shiyeh. I am here, above you. Don't be scared and don't worry. We will get you out from here with Hashem's help. Don't feel guilty. Don't answer me. Just listen to my instructions – and follow them. Keep all your strength right now. Be very careful when you move and do whatever I tell you."

Rabbi Shiyeh began lowering the rope towards Shuki. "Listen carefully," he called down the cliff. "I am lowering an improvised rope to you. I do not intend to pull you up with the rope, because I am not certain that it will be strong enough to support you. The purpose of the rope is only to give you more confidence. More protection. As soon as the rope reaches you, you should very, very carefully lift one hand from the plants you are holding onto and grab hold of the rope."

A few moments later we heard Rabbi Shiyeh continue to guide Shuki, trying his best to sound calm and controlled. "Carefully… yes, carefully… wonderful! Grab the strong rope… wind it around your hand a few times. Carefully… excellent! Now, grab hold of the plants again like before. Try to raise your feet to the most stable place you can find."

Our principal was risking his life on the edge of the waterfall in order to maintain eye-contact with Shuki. He continued to calm and encourage him. At the same time, five of our classmates sat on the ground, tightly holding the end of a rope made out of our shirts. As for the rest of us, what exactly were we supposed to do?

We huddled together and began to recite chapters of *Tehillim*. Dudi had a pocket sized edition of *Tehillim* in his wallet and he now became the *chazzen* – we repeated after him.

Lamnatzeiach mizmor le-dovid...

Ya'anchoh Hashem be-yom tzoroh...

Yishlach ezrecha mi-kodesh...

Hashem hoshiah, ha-melech ya'aneinu ve-yom korenu...

We pleaded with all our might. With my entire being, I begged and hoped that Shuki would not slip, *chas ve'sholom*, and we would not have to put the strength of our "rope" and five classmates to the test...

"Oh no!!" A frightened cry burst from the lips of our five classmates who were holding the upper end of the rope. We looked at them with our hearts pounding. The rope was stretched out to its fullest. Clearly, Shuki's grip on the plants had come loose and he was dangling on the side of the cliff. His entire body was now supported only by our shirts...

At the same time, we heard the voice of Rabbi Shiyeh. "Shuki, calm down. Don't lose your focus. Hold tightly to the rope."

From where we were, we could not see Shuki, but the situation was clear enough – and incredibly frightening.

I closed my eyes and concentrated on praying. *Shir ha-ma'alos, esa einai el he-harim, mei'ayin yovo ezri...* How very appropriate those words now seemed...

Ezri mei'im Hashem, osei shomayim vo'oretz... I was prepared to sacrifice anything as long as Shuki would get out of there in one piece.

Al yitein lamot raglecha... My heart threatened to explode when for a second the image of the rope snapping and Shuki plunging down the rocky cliff flashed before my eyes. I quickly tried to erase that awful image from my mind and continued reciting *Tehillim* in a loud voice and with intense concentration. *Hashem shomrecha. Hashem tzil'cha al yad yeminecha... Hashem yishmorecha mikol ra, yishmor es nafshecha...*

I sensed that my cheeks were moist and realized that I was crying. It did not bother me and I was not in the least embarrassed. In such terrible distress there can be no room for petty calculations. Anyway, I sensed that all of my friends thought and felt exactly the same way as I did.

We suddenly heard the sound of a faint rumbling. As we listened, it grew stronger and nearer. "A helicopter!" someone called out excitedly. It was true. A rescue helicopter was soon hovering over our heads. Chills spread across my whole body. Have you ever heard the expression "racing against the clock?" Well, that was now the reality. The question was: Could the rescue team reach Shuki before his strength gave out or the improvised rope came apart?

I continued reciting words of *Tehillim*, my body trembling and my eyes wet from the unbearable anxiety of the moment.

• • •

The helicopter drew close to the waterfall. The door opened and a member of the rescue team emerged and began to lower himself

down on a cable to where Shuki was grasping the makeshift rope with his last ounce of strength.

We could not see Shuki, as I mentioned earlier, but we could see Rabbi Rosen standing far below at the foot of the waterfall. He was using a cell phone and with wide sweeps of his arm guided the helicopter from below.

The roar of the helicopter rotors was deafening. We hald onto our *yarmulkes* as the wind generated by its propellers almost blew us away.

Rabbi Shiyeh rose from his position at the edge of the cliff. The helicompter's rotating blades and powerful blast generated additional danger for him.

"Continue *davening*!" he called towards us. "Continue, until with Hashem's help, we see Shuki standing on firm ground, healthy and whole!" He was screaming loud enough for us to hear through the din of the helicopter and the roar of the waterfall. It seemed to me that new creases had formed along Rabbi Shiyeh's forehead. I was now able to appreciate the burden and responsibility that he carried.

The rescue mission persisted. My heart continued to pound heavily.

Suddenly, I saw the rescuer and Shuki being drawn up by the cable. Shuki's face was as white as a sheet. He was being held by a special harness and his face showed signs of fright.

My friends and I waved to him, but he did not even look our way. It was so strange to see Shuki this way.

After several moments, Shuki was swallowed into the cabin of the helicopter which then rose upwards on an angle. Just a few seconds later, it touched down in an open parking lot not too far from us.

Rabbi Rosen and Rabbi Levin joined us and we all hurried over to the parking lot. We were desperate to see Shuki and be reassured that he was alright.

The pilot turned off the motor. The blades continued to rotate from the power of their momentum. To our great surprise, Shuki did not run towards us in joy as we imagined he would. In fact, he did not even stand on his feet. Shuki was carried out of the helicopter on a stretcher.

We were not allowed to approach the helicopter. Only Rabbi Shiyeh approached and spoke briefly with the team.

"Well," he addressed us with a slightly concerned face when he returned to where we were waiting, "there is good news and not so good news. The good news is that Shuki was rescued and is still with us, *Boruch Hashem*... The not so good news is that Shuki seems to have broken his right leg when he fell and now requires medical treatment."

Rabbi Shiyeh spoke privately with the two teachers. He seemed to be giving them instructions for the remainder of the evening. He then returned to the rescue team and assisted them in filling out a detailed form regarding the incident. They shook hands and Rabbi Shiyeh left them. He then accompanied Shuki in a taxi to a hospital for examination and medical care.

We left in the four jeeps that were waiting for us in the parking lot, bouncing our way towards Katzrin for the night. We had to prepare for the second day of our grand trip. The trip now had a strange atmosphere. On one hand, it was a wonderful trip and we had thoroughly enjoyed every moment of it, including traveling in half-opened jeeps. On the other hand, we were still under the powerful influence of the frightening events of the waterfall. Also, the uncertain condition of Shuki, and the fact that the principal was forced to leave us, temporarily weighed on our hearts. Elimelech did not travel in the same jeep as me, but I am confident that he was not feeling too good after what happened.

Rabbi Rosen and Rabbi Levin worked skillfully to return the trip to the same sense of joy that pervaded it until the incident at the waterfall. We came to our camp grounds at Katzrin and settled in a giant tent that had been prepared for us. We rinsed our hands and faces and *davened maariv*. Our teachers informed us that a surprise awaited us immediately after *davening*.

The surprise turned out to be a nighttime "*kumzitz*." Rabbi Rosen and Rabbi Levin brought us to a nearby forest clearing where a large circle of smoothened rocks had been positioned for sitting on. At the center of the circle there was a pit filled with coals. A metal grate had been placed above them for barbecuing. One of the jeeps approached us with large baskets containing a variety of meats, cut vegetables and light drinks.

It was a most wonderful surprise. Soon we were sitting in a circle, eating heartily, while the coals flickered and lit up the night. The air was clean and pleasant, the sky shimmered with stars, and the atmosphere seemed magical.

At a certain point, Rabbi Rosen turned around and opened a small black box that he had kept behind him. He fiddled with something for a few moments. He turned back to face us, holding… a clarinet! We were shocked, stunned. We had absolutely no idea

that Rabbi Rosen was musical. He placed one end of the clarinet by his mouth and wonderful sounds emerged, pouring into the night's air. At first, he played a pleasant, calm tune, a little sad, perhaps. We did not recognize the melody, but it was so very moving that we all listened as if we had been hypnotized. Then he began playing familiar tunes. We joined in with singing. It was an extremely heartwarming evening.

After a quarter of an hour of singing and music, Rabbi Levin asked for silence – he had something to say.

"Dear students," he began, "there is a Yiddish saying: *Ah mentch tracht un G-t lacht*. Basically, that means that a person sits and plans and makes all sorts of arrangements, but Hashem hears him planning – and laughs at it. Only He knows just how far those plans are from the reality that He has already prepared for that person.

"We set out yesterday morning for a two-day hiking trip. Little could we imagine the dramatic and tense moments that awaited us. *Boruch Hashem*, those moments ended with kindness and mercy, and they are now behind us. However, since we believe that everything that occurs is designed by Hashem, we must therefore analyze every event in our lives and draw a moral conclusion from it. There is more than one lesson to be drawn from today's experience."

We listened to Rabbi Levin's words in a silence that was punctured only by the crackling of the flaming coals and the calls of the various species of bats that flew over our heads.

"For a start, we must make sure to listen and carefully obey the instructions of those responsible for us. See what happens when we are disobedient and do things without permission...?

"Secondly, and perhaps this is the most important point, we saw the close friendship that emerges when one of us falls into distress. What warm prayers we offer for his sake! How many tears we shed for our friend! This all teaches us that in a moment of truth – we are all one family."

Rabbi Levin gave a sigh. "Why, then, must we wait until one of us is in extreme danger, *chas ve'sholom*? Why not express the same amazing friendship when everything is going well?"

His words touched my heart. I greatly identified with them.

The wonderful evening continued. We sang, spoke, laughed, made a series of skits, and even danced.

What can I say? In all of my nine years learning in *cheder*, I do not remember such a unique atmosphere filled with friendship and unity.

Towards the end of the *kumzitz*, the principal returned. He told us that Shuki's right foot had been put in a cast and that Shuki had been sent home.

The remainder of the trip, was pleasant and filled with good and pleasurable experiences. What made the event completely unforgettable, as I mentioned at the start, was the incident at the waterfall and the night *kumzitz* that followed. It was the kind of experience that you carry with you for the rest of your life.

Entering Yeshivah

We have less than two months left until the summer break – what they call *bein hazemanim* in *yeshivah* language. Right after that, we will be entering *yeshivah.*

What excitement! What suspense! Some nights, I have difficulty falling asleep because my mind is so preoccupied with thoughts of *yeshivah* and what awaits me there.

Most of my classmates will split between the three central and well-known *yeshivos*. A few students have enrolled in other, smaller less-known institutions. Some boys are going to the same *yeshivah* in which their older brothers studied. I certainly will not have that privilege, because… well, I do not have an older brother.

Do you remember that I told you about my parents' dilemma as to which institution I should enroll in?

In the end, my father was convinced of my mother's position, and with Hashem's help, I will be entering a prominent *yeshivah*, despite its more distant location from our home. It takes an hour to travel there. My mother insisted that we could not compare present conditions to the situation in which my father found himself when he was a boy.

"Nowadays," she insisted, "there are telephones easily available, and quick, accessible transportation in every location. We can easily visit the kid on a regular basis." (I found it amusing to overhear my parents talking together and referring to me as "the kid"...)

In school, our class is bubbling with excitement and anticipation at the approaching conclusion of the school year. We are proud to be entering *yeshivah*. We discuss our upcoming transition constantly, analyzing the issues from every angle as if it were a profound debate in the *Gemara*.

• • •

Three days passed since our grand trip and Shuki had still not shown his face in the classroom. It was somewhat surprising because he lives just two houses away from our school building. True, his foot was in a cast, but could he not use crutches and if need be, a wheelchair?

During the afternoon recess, Nachum and I decided to go together to fulfill the *mitzvah* of visiting the sick.

We met Shuki in the garden of his house. He was sitting on a rocking chair and reading a book. His leg was in a cast and was stretched out straight in front of him. A pair of crutches lay one on top of the other at his side. When he noticed us, he folded the corner of the page to keep his place and straightened himself a little.

"We came to see how our daredevil friend is doing!" I called out in an attempt to create a light atmosphere.

"That was nice of you," Shuki answered with a smile.

We sat beside him on two white plastic chairs that we dragged from another corner of the yard and asked him how his foot was doing. He was forced to keep it in a cast for another month and a half because of the angle of the fracture. But in just three weeks, the length of the cast would be reduced, making it significantly easier for him to move around.

"Tell me something," Nachum suddenly blurted out. "What exactly were you thinking when you came so close to the edge of the cliff, huh? What on earth were you looking for up there – apart from trouble…?"

Nachum tends to ask extremely direct and pointed questions, without predicting their embarrassing results.

"What was I thinking?" Shuki repeated his question. "What was I looking for?

"Hmmm… I don't really know."

Shuki looked like he was now terribly embarrassed by what he had done and the whole drama that it had caused.

"Truth is…" he added after thinking for another moment, "I think that I really do know what I was thinking and what I was looking for up there. What I was looking for was this: That… everyone should look at me and pay attention to me..."

"Ah!" chuckled Nachum, but I was puzzled.

"You just don't understand..." replied Shuki, with a look of frustration over his face. "I knew that you would not understand me..." he added in a choked voice.

"What are you trying to say, Shuki?" I attempted to understand. "Please explain yourself. I promise to at least try to understand."

Shuki did not hurry to reply.

It seemed as if he was trying to decide whether he should share with us what pained him, something that he had already hinted to.

"Okay, I will try to explain it to you," Shuki eventually consented. "That's because I consider both of you to be good and intelligent friends. But whatever we discuss here must remain between us – you guarantee?"

We assured him and he began:

"Look – I do not know whether you paid attention, but it has been a long while since I have performed any pranks. I have also greatly progressed in my studies. I may not be one of the most outstanding students in our class, but you can certainly say that I improved. By the way, do you know who helped me accomplish this? Elimelech. For the past two and a half months, Elimelech has been my study partner each evening after school."

That's nice of Elimelech, I thought to myself. Shuki threw us a glance, trying to read our reaction from our looks. We listened with great attention as he spoke.

"However, it seems that all of this did not help me when I took examination tests in order to enroll in a *yeshivah*. I applied to four *yeshivos*! I have already been examined by three of them. Weeks have passed and not one *yeshivah* has responded positively. My feeling is that I have already acquired a reputation as an incurable troublemaker, and it doesn't matter that I have changed...

"I sit in the classroom and hear everyone discussing their upcoming entry into *yeshivah* with sparkling eyes, while I feel cut off from the whole experience – I still do not have a *yeshivah* to attend! You are all happy and excited. I am left with nothing but loneliness and despair. You have to understand… my parents are simple people who have no connections with any of the *yeshivos*. They can't open any doors for me."

Two streams of tears suddenly burst from Shuki's eyes. He quickly wiped them away with the back of his hand.

At first, we were astonished. We had no idea what to say. Instinctively, I placed my hand on Shuki's shoulder. It was difficult for me to come to terms with the fact that such sadness and painful loneliness lurked behind Shuki's mischievous and cheerful conduct.

"Do you understand?" Shuki continued after he had calmed down a bit. "That's what I meant when I said that I was looking for everyone to look at me and pay attention to me. I thought that if inside the classroom I felt non-existent and irrelevant, then at least I wanted to stand out during the hike – to do something for all our friends."

A painful silence filled the yard. A small pinecone fell from the fir tree that sheltered us. It landed directly on the end of my shoe, then bounced and rolled away. It was now completely obvious why Shuki was not rushing to get back to the classroom. Even without the cast on his foot, he felt very bad.

"And what exactly were you thinking?" Nachum once again weighed in bluntly. "Did you imagine that if you would cause mischief during the trip, then your reputation would improve dramatically? That your new, outstanding reputation would quickly reach the ears of the *yeshivah* administration? I am just trying to work out your logic..."

Shuki lowered his eyes. "You are right…" he mumbled. His tears threatened to break their way out once more. "I felt pushed into a corner and had to do something, anything, just to find a way of expression."

"Tell me something," I turned to Shuki. "Are the teachers and the principal aware of this? Has anyone informed them about your situation?"

Shuki placed his hand beneath his cast in an attempt to move his leg slightly. He seemed to be buying time. "No," he eventually replied. "In fact, they have asked me and showed interest, but I was always too ashamed to admit the truth. I preferred to tell them that I was in touch with a number of *yeshivos* and that we are still undecided..."

"Listen, friends," Nachum called out in a decisive tone. I noticed the sparkle of determination in his eyes. I recognized that look. When Nachum has that sparkle, he intends to do something important – to undertake some truly vital task.

"Listen well," Nachum looked directly into Shuki's eyes. "With Hashem's help, you will enter a *yeshivah*!"

A confused smile broke across Shuki's lips. "What... What do you mean?" he stammered.

"We will take care of it," Nachum declared firmly and winked towards me to include me in the "we."

"We will work with whoever we need to, and will not rest or be quiet until you have been accepted into a *yeshivah*."

Shuki beamed. His two eyes shone like rays of sunlight breaking through grey clouds. He struggled to find words to express his emotion.

"Then my strategy worked, huh?" he joked, his mischievous look returning. "Just as I told you – I climbed up to the top of the cliff in order to draw attention, and now someone has finally noticed me…!"

• • •

Nachum decided to strike while the iron was hot. Immediately after the afternoon recess he asked Rabbi Levin for permission to "bring an urgent topic" to the attention of the class.

Rabbi Levin could not imagine what Nachum was referring to, but his reply showed that he trusted Nachum's judgment. "Go ahead and enlighten us," he declared in an encouraging tone.

"Do you remember all of those heartfelt prayers that we offered on Shuki's behalf during the hike?" Nachum began with a question that immediately silenced the whispers of a curious class. Without waiting for a reply to his rhetorical question, Nachum marched on, "And do you remember what Rabbi Levin told us that evening – that we must not wait until a time of trouble to show a friend our love and friendship?"

Everyone nodded, trying to guess what he was getting at. Even Rabbi Levin looked a little tense. "You remember," Nachum confirmed the obvious. "Very well," he added, glancing quickly around the room at all of his friends.

"In that case," he continued, "we now have an opportunity to truly test our sense of friendship. To determine whether we truly internalized the message from the incident at the waterfall."

Nachum then informed our classmates about the visit that he and I paid to Shuki just a short while earlier. The comments it elicited from the class showed a broad range of emotions.

"Can it be true?" Yoki muttered in complete shock.

"I would never have believed it!" Chaim responded.

"Oh, how very sad…" sighed Meni. It was clear from looking at him that he was truly pained.

"In fact, I *had* noticed that he was a little distant from us lately…" Dudi exclaimed.

For the next couple of minutes, each classmate in turn expressed his feelings about Shuki's predicament.

"What you have told us here is certainly painful," Rabbi Levin interrupted the class debate. "The fact is… I have tried time and again to extract a clear answer from Shuki as to his plans for the coming year. He has always avoided answering me clearly."

A minute later Rabbi Levin added, "There is an expression: 'One action is better than a thousand sighs.' All of our sighing and sympathizing will not do Shuki any good. If someone here has an idea as to how we can actually help Shuki, then I would be pleased to hear it."

As soon as he said that, all eyes turned to Elimelech, who until then had sat silently and not joined the class discussion at all. Elimelech, as I noted earlier, is Shuki's closest friend. It was only natural that everyone expected him to have something to say at such a time.

"Why are you all staring at me?" Elimelech protested, and he blushed.

"Because you are Shuki's closest friend and you know him better than the rest of us," I answered Elimelech gently.

Elimelech lowered his eyes as if he was accepting the judgment. "Okay," he finally announced. "The truth is that I knew all of this for weeks already, but Shuki made me promise not to tell anyone – and I stood by my word to him. But now that you all are aware of his situation, I don't think that there is anything preventing me from participating in your discussion, for Shuki's benefit..."

Elimelech sounded emotional, which was unusual for him. "It's a bit of a secret…" he said, lowering his voice. "Recently, we began studying together in the evenings. We alternate: One night we study in Shuki's house, the next in my own. I can tell you that the six pages of *Gemara* that we are all examined on for entry to *yeshivah* – Shuki knows them backwards and forwards. Shuki's problem is that he becomes very nervous every time he goes for an examination and that prevents him from communicating his true knowledge of the material. When you add that to the reputation that he had made for himself over the years, he then has a real problem…"

I was impressed by the mature manner in which Elimelech expressed and analyzed the issue.

"One day, I approached Shuki with an original suggestion," Elimelech continued. He then fell quiet. He seemed to be hesitating, unsure whether it was proper to reveal personal details about Shuki. "Okay… I don't know… Shuki might not want me…" he mumbled out loud.

Nachum pressed him to continue. "This is for Shuki's sake," he reminded Elimelech. "He is screaming for our help."

"Okay," Elimelech agreed. "So, one day, I told Shuki that my father regularly gives large donations to one of the *yeshivos* in which Shuki was examined. I suggested to him that my father involve himself on his behalf and try to apply pressure on the administration in order to get him accepted."

"Wonderful!" Chaim could not contain himself.

"Excellent idea!" Itzik agreed.

"Well, you say 'wonderful' and 'excellent,'" Elimelech hurried to cool their enthusiasm, "but Shuki didn't think that way at all. He forbade me from involving my father in the matter. 'No way! Don't you dare do that!' Shuki warned me. 'I will carry an awful feeling for the rest of my life to know that on my part, I was unfit for *yeshivah*, but because someone gave the *yeshivah* a lot of money, the administration did me a favor and allowed me in...' Shuki was completely against the idea."

I felt that the discussion about Shuki had somehow bonded the class. This was not the sort of talk designed to mix into someone else's problems. It was a serious discussion that stemmed from our deep desire to help Shuki.

Rabbi Levin listened to the discussion while deep in his own thoughts. "Very well, friends," he announced at last. "We are going to end this important discussion for now. I suggest that each of you continue to rethink this matter and then tomorrow, after the afternoon recess, we will again consider the ideas that you raise."

A serious expression crossed Rabbi Levin's face. "There is one more thing that I want to ask from you. Since our intention is good and pure, and since we are not interested in causing any embarrassment, *chas ve'sholom*, we must keep this discussion a complete secret. Do not discuss it in public. Do not allow anyone who is not present right now to find out about it. Letting out the secret will have serious consequences on what we are trying to accomplish."

• • •

"Good for you," I patted Nachum on the shoulder on the way home from school.

"Wait a little with the compliment," he replied with a half-smile. "First let's see if we can succeed… I feel that we simply must do something about this. For Shuki's sake. For all of our sakes."

"You know what?" Nachum added, his eyes staring at some place in the distance. "I have the feeling that the pages of *Gemara* and its commentaries that we studied for the entrance exam was only part of our test – the written test. But the true test that will make us fit to be accepted will be if and when we succeed in arranging that Shuki is accepted into a *yeshivah*."

Thoughts of Shuki did not leave me alone at night, while I was lying in bed. I had never considered him among my especially close friends, but now I yearned with all my heart to help him.

The pain that he projected, his crying and even his foot in a cast – it all caused me to feel strong pangs of concern, pity, and friendship towards him.

With these thoughts still swirling in my mind, I finally fell asleep.

Shuki was absent from school the next day as well. That was a good thing, because as expected, his predicament continued to occupy us. We reviewed his situation at every opportunity. All sorts of wild ideas were thrown into the air. We waited impatiently for Rabbi Levin's arrival following the afternoon recess. We hoped that with his help we would succeed in pinpointing the idea that will get Shuki accepted to a *yeshivah*.

Once again, it was Nachum who broached the topic. "We would like to remind you, rebbi… we came up with all sorts of ideas…"

"You do not need to remind me," Rabbi Levin replied in a quiet and serious voice. "Since yesterday, he has not left my head for even a second." He smiled and added, "Well? Let's hear what ideas you have managed to pull out of your hats."

One after another, we presented our thoughts. Some of them were quite original.

Yoki, for example, suggested publicizing the names of the outstanding students in the class in a local newspaper and including Shuki's name. "That way, his reputation will improve," he explained.

Dudi also came up with an interesting idea: "We need to arrange for Shuki to receive a repeat-test in one of the *yeshivos*, but this time he will be permitted to take a written test, not the standard oral exam. Then he won't be as nervous and will be able to demonstrate how well he really knows his stuff."

After a half hour of discussion, Rabbi Levin stood up and began pacing back and forth in the classroom while stroking his beard. That is what he does whenever his mind is busy cooking up a plan. He came to a halt opposite Elimelech's table.

"Remind me, please: Which *yeshivah* are you going to?" he questioned. Elimelech named one of the best and most sought-after *yeshivos*.

"And was Shuki already examined by this *yeshivah*?" Rabbi Levin asked.

"No, he did not apply to this *yeshivah*," answered Elimelech.

Both the question and answer were unnecessary, because this was one of the most difficult *yeshivos* to enroll in.

"Excellent," Rabbi Levin announced and returned to his seat.

"Okay," he addressed the class, "Tell me what you think about the following plan..." He removed his glasses and rapidly rubbed his eyes. "What do you think about this? We will try to arrange that in a few days from now we will pay a class visit to the home of Rabbi Levitensky. He is the head of the *yeshivah* in which Elimelech will be studying next year. The *rosh yeshivah* does not live far from our neighborhood. We will ask him to test us on the pages of *Gemara* that you have all prepared for your *yeshivah* entrance exams. It is common practice for classes to have themselves examined towards the end of a school year by a famous Rabbi or *rosh yeshivah*..."

We were surprised. The concept sounded fine, but how was it connected with Shuki?

"What don't you understand?" Rabbi Levin read our thoughts. "Shuki will also be present and we will make sure that he creates a good impression on the *rosh yeshivah*."

We did not fully understand our teacher's plan, but knew that we could rely on him.

"We just have to hope that Shuki comes back to class before then," Chaim pointed out half-jokingly.

"You can leave the technical details to me," Rabbi Levin replied, and he too, smiled.

• • •

Our visit to the home of Rabbi Levitensky took place approximately one week later.

Oh – I forgot to mention that Shuki finally returned to class. For some reason, Shuki now seemed far more relaxed and encouraged. Perhaps it had to do with the fact that his foot was healing faster than expected and his cast had been reduced in size earlier than planned. He was now able to move more easily, although he still required crutches. I probably do not need to tell you that no one mentioned a thing to him about the discussions we held in his absence.

Getting back to our visit at the home of the *rosh yeshivah*… It was very moving indeed. Rabbi Levitensky welcomed us in at the doorway to his home, shaking the hands of each boy in turn. When he saw Shuki hopping on his crutches, he declared, "Look at that! What sacrifice for the sake of studying Torah! He comes with a broken foot and crutches…" He accompanied Shuki into his home with a merciful look on his face. Out of respect for Shuki's condition, Rabbi Levitensky had him sit right next to him at the table.

"So, what have you been studying recently?" the *rosh yeshivah* asked with interest. Rabbi Levin presented a few words by way of general introduction, first about our *cheder* and then about the subject we were studying. Rabbi Levitensky then removed a volume of *Gemara – Baba Kama* – from the enormous set of bookshelves behind him, opened it to the chapter *Hachovel*, and began asking us questions. The questions were not too difficult, and the atmosphere was very relaxed.

Rabbi Levin controlled the event. The *rosh yeshivah* would ask a question and then Rabbi Levin would choose a student to answer it. Rabbi Levin directed the first question to Shuki, who did not get confused and returned a quick and clear answer. After another three questions to other students, Rabbi Levin again directed a question to Shuki. Once again Shuki provided an excellent and clear answer. This pattern was repeated throughout the exam – after every three or four questions, it went back to Shuki.

The truth is that I was surprised at Shuki's knowledge. This was certainly not the same Shuki that I had known.

If a stranger would have walked into the room, he would have been immediately convinced that Shuki was the best and brightest student in the class. That was also the impression he made on the *rosh yeshivah*. It was obvious to everyone. After the fourth or fifth answer that Shuki supplied, the *rosh yeshivah* could barely contain his excitement.

"I do not know which *yeshivah* you have chosen to enroll in next year," he said to Shuki, leaning a hand on Shuki's shoulder, "but whichever *yeshivah* gets you will be lucky indeed!"

Shuki beamed like the sun. He could not believe this was happening to him. He suddenly found himself raised from the lowest, most desperate situation to the very top of the mountain! At that moment, my eyes met Nachum's. He seemed to be as moved as Shuki was. In fact, it was all to his credit. If it were not for his concern and initiative, it is quite likely that Shuki would still be sitting at home in pain.

I will spare you all the details and get straight to the bottom line: Shuki was accepted into the *yeshivah* of Rabbi Levitensky without requiring another exam. The knowledge that he displayed at the home of the *rosh yeshivah* was sufficient. As for a study partner in *yeshivah*, he did not have to search hard to find one; he already had one prepared – his closest friend Elimelech.

• • •

Now, my good friends, it has come time for us to go our separate ways.

In just another few weeks, I will enter *yeshivah*. I suspect that I will need to take a long break from writing to you. At first, at least, keeping pace in *yeshivah* will demand every possible moment.

I am delighted at the opportunity that you have provided me to share some personal experiences during one of the most important and decisive years of my life. I also hope that you have absorbed the messages that I have tried to impart through the episodes that I shared.

As our *chachomim* state, "Do not look at the jar, but at its contents." Do not judge someone by his external, superficial appearance alone. You must also look at a person's inner self and experience. As the *Mishneh* continues: "There could be a brand new jar filled with old wine, or an ancient jar filled with fresh wine." In other words: Always look at the third dimension as well. That is, the depth.

Goodbye!

I hope to meet you again sometime.

In honor of our
dear children:

Chana, Leah, Bayla, Mushka,
Naomi and Moishe

you continue to make us proud
Mommy and Tatty

לע״נ

האשה החשובה

מרת **שיינדל** ב״ר **יצחק** ע״ה

אוד מוצל מאש

נלב״ע ג׳ שבט תשע״ג

ת.נ.צ.ב.ה.

לע"נ

ר' **יוסף** בן ר' **שלמה** ז"ל

נפטר י"ח סיון תשע"א

לזכות בנו ומשפחתו שיחיו

נדפס ע"י נכדו

הרה"ת ר' **יעקב זאב** וזוגתו **מעיין**

ילדיהם: **חנה, לוי יצחק,**

משה חיים ואודל

אלבליה שיחיו

להצלחה בגו"ר

In honor of our
dear children:
Mussy, Dovid, and Chanale
may you always give us
much Nachas

לע"נ

ר' **טובי'** ב"ר **משה** ז"ל

וזוגתו **חנהביילא**

בת ר' **משולם זוסיא** ז"ל

לזכות כל יו"ח שיחיו

לע"נ

האשה החשובה

מרת **פיגא ציפא** ע"ה

בת ר' **יהושע** הי"ד

לאופר

נפטרה עש"ק י"ד שבט תשע"ג

ת.נ.צ.ב.ה.

Made in the USA
Middletown, DE
24 August 2021

46809207R00121